To all of my students, who have made my chosen profession one of some frustration and many rewards. Teaching has certainly never been dull.

To my principal, colleagues, and friends who have encouraged me in and shared the fun of this venture.

ABOUT THE AUTHOR

Sharon Neumayr teaches English at Central High School in Pueblo, Colorado, where she has a special interest in sponsoring the National Honor Society and in coaching the academic teams. Formerly she taught English in Minnesota. Ms. Neumayr holds a B.S. in education and an M.A. in literature. She is a member of local, state, and national education associations and the National Council of Teachers of English, and she has been actively involved in civic organizations.

Sharon Motsenbocker

AMERICAN LITERATURE ACTIVITIES KIT

READY-TO-USE WORKSHEETS FOR SECONDARY STUDENTS

AMERICAN LITERATURE ACTIVITIES KIT

READY-TO-USE WORKSHEETS FOR SECONDARY STUDENTS

SHARON NEUMAYR

Illustrated by Marc Vargas

THE CENTER FOR APPLIED
RESEARCH IN EDUCATION
West Nyack, New York 10995

Library of Congress Cataloging-in-Publication Data

Neumayr, Sharon, 1942–
American literature activities kit / Sharon Neumayr.
p. cm.
ISBN 0-87628-110-2
1. American literature—Study and teaching (Secondary)
2. Activity programs in education. I. Title.
PS42.N48 1992 91-5094
810′.71′273—dc20 CIP

Printed in the United States of America
10 9 8 7 6 5

ISBN 0-87628-110-2

THE CENTER FOR APPLIED RESEARCH IN EDUCATION
West Nyack, NY 10994
A Simon & Schuster Company

On the World Wide Web at http://www.phdirect.com

Prentice-Hall International (UK) Limited, *London*
Prentice-Hall of Australia Pty. Limited, *Sydney*
Prentice-Hall Canada Inc., *Toronto*
Prentice-Hall Hispanoamericana, S.A., *Mexico*
Prentice-Hall of India Private Limited, *New Delhi*
Prentice-Hall of Japan, Inc., *Tokyo*
Simon & Schuster Asia Pte. Ltd., *Singapore*
Editora Prentice-Hall do Brasil, Ltda., *Rio de Janeiro*

ABOUT THIS RESOURCE

To me, reading—*lots* of reading—is still the best way to understand and appreciate American literature. However, activities and projects can help make this literature come alive for students. *American Literature Activities Kit* is a collection of over 145 activities that have worked for me. Each activity is ready to use, which will save you preparation time.

Organized into seven chronological sections that follow the typical American literature curriculum, the kit can be used with most secondary students (it is especially suitable for grades 9–12). The activities were designed for a variety of interests and ability levels and range from fairly easy spelling games to rather complex literary analysis. Each section has a consistent format: it begins with a skills index, worksheet notes and answers, project ideas, a reproducible chronology, and a reproducible bibliography. Reproducible worksheets then form the core of each section.

Far more than "busy work," these worksheets were designed to encourage independent and critical thinking and creativity, to develop students' historical perspective, and to reinforce important skills. Their use is intended to be flexible. Most can be used as individual or class activities; they may serve as a basis for discussions, projects, and oral or written reports. Many can be used for more than one unit. For example, students often enjoy doing "A Day in the Life" from Section 1 at a later stage in their studies so they can compare lifestyle changes over time. And the United States map in the first section can be used throughout the study of American literature.

Since a true understanding of American literature requires historical perspective, several activities in each section ask students to see how past incidents and beliefs affect us today. Or, students may be asked to "become" a literary or historical character—for instance, a young person trying to decide whether to set sail on the Mayflower, or the parishioner of a Puritan preacher.

For much of my teaching career it appeared that there were either no women in the colonies or that those who were there exerted no influence and had no thoughts of their own. To remedy that, this resource contains a number of activities that remind students not only of the contributions of women but also of the contributions of various ethnic groups and regions of the country.

Each of the seven sections contains work that will reinforce basic skills. Literary skills are the focus of several worksheets in each section. Students note how authors do their work, and they then try their hand at the literary devices being studied. They write similes and metaphors, discover and explain allusions, track the plot pattern of a short story, or decide what rhyme adds to a poem.

Three to five activities in each section are directed toward spelling and vocabulary skills. A reproducible vocabulary list of seventy-five words is offered in each section, drawing on literature characteristic of the period. Many of these vocabulary words are also on the list often used to study for the PSAT and SAT tests, and with that in mind, one worksheet in each chapter gives students practice in working with analogies. Students also work with synonyms, antonyms, prefixes, and suffixes, as well as exercises designed to show the growth of American English.

Composition skills play a part in many of the activities, but several are solely for the practice of expository, descriptive, and persuasive writing, becoming slightly more advanced as students proceed through the year. Style, sentence structure, word choice, and parallel structure are some of the topics discussed. Skills required to understand the different types of writing in a newspaper also make up a part of each chapter. Many activities call for students to use specific thinking skills, such as inductive and deductive reasoning, generalizing, classifying, synthesizing, drawing conclusions, and problem solving.

The appendix contains a list of suggested authors for each era and an index to worksheets by literary skill taught.

I hope the ideas and activities in *American Literature Activities Kit* add to your store of "tricks of the trade." If this book helps you, I am grateful. Perhaps it is one way I can repay all the teachers and colleagues who have helped me during my years in the classroom.

Sharon Neumayr

CONTENTS

Vocabulary Skills

APPENDIX

AMERICAN LITERATURE ACTIVITIES KIT

READY-TO-USE WORKSHEETS FOR SECONDARY STUDENTS

Section 1
THE COLONIAL ERA

1492-1760 Columbus to Franklin

SKILLS INDEX

WORKSHEET NOTES

1-1. It Happened Where?

1-2. A Whole Land Beyond

In addition to exercising the map-reading, spatial, and chronological thinking skills built into these worksheets, students are asked to see that history is made up of interrelated incidents. In combining these skills with literature, students should see that great historical events were brought about by living, breathing people subject to the same weaknesses and frailties that we are today. They were no different than any of us who are trying to make our way as best we can. We, too, are part of history in the making.

1-3. To Go—or Not to Go

The story of immigration to the New Land is a great adventure story. The colonists had courage, the strength of their convictions, and tenacity. Nevertheless, the decision to leave one's homeland is never an easy one. This worksheet should help students understand how difficult the decision must have been in most cases.

1-4. Mayflower Moving

To do this worksheet students need to keep in mind the following concerning their reading from this era:

—the size of the Mayflower and number of passengers
—type of clothing and climate
—religious beliefs
—dangers at sea and on land
—lifestyle; type of work to be done on arrival
—geography
—natives

The students should then do their best to be the young immigrant.

1-5. A Day in the Life

Here students will put themselves in the place of a colonial woman. Once they think about the normal work expected of this woman and plot the time it may have taken, the students should have a much better understanding of the lives of our founding fathers and mothers. Also, historically speaking, three hundred to four hundred years isn't such a long time. Once again, this exercise may help these people come alive for the students.

1-6. The Promise and the Reality

1-7. Then and Now

Our cultural history as a country began in the sixteenth and seventeenth centuries. It is often difficult for students to understand how past events affect our lives today. Through these worksheets they will see this and also realize that literature makes that history and culture live.

1-8. A Rousing Sermon

This is another exercise in role playing. The God of the Puritans and Pilgrims has permeated the culture and institutions of the United States throughout its history. An awareness of this will help students understand much in history and in present-day life.

1-9. North and South

Students are lead gently to the writing of a three-paragraph expository composition in which they compare and contrast in several areas. A few of the possible topics are listed here.

Similarities

—hardships, such as lack of food, illness, climate
—often fiercely independent
—importance of religious beliefs
—spirit of adventure
—same native land
—Native Americans

Differences

—climate harsher in the North
—family backgrounds of the leaders
—geography
—reasons for settling:
South—often economics
North—religion
—South—people often more comfort-
—able financially
—politics—loyalties in the South generally to the Crown (note the place names)
—South—more forced immigration; little in the North

1-10. The Best Things in Life

Assigning a student a persuasive composition can be a daunting prospect for both teacher and student. This is one way to sneak up on them. Later they can be told just what they did, and the characteristics of persuasion can be discussed.

1-11. They Said It Their Way

All of us describe things for others. However, many people are unaware of how their speaking and writing styles, of which word choice is a part, express a philosophy concerning the subject. This exercise may be a bit difficult for some students, but the results should prove worth the struggle.

1-12. Rhyme Time

Poetry uses rhyme. Allowing students to think about rhyme in a particular poem places them in the position of the poet. If their answers are "off the wall," it is all right for now. Further exercise will allow them to become more proficient with poetic devices.

1-13. It's a What?!?

1-14. Worth a Thousand Words

1-15. Onomatopoeia

These worksheets are designed to show how authors do their work, how they can say so much with few words. Metaphors, similes, and onomatopoeia can be fun when shared with the rest of the class. Colonial literature is replete with allusions to Greek and Roman mythology, Seneca, Socrates, Chaucer, and the Bible, to name a few. For example, in *The History of Plymouth Plantation,* Bradford alludes to the Roman poet Seneca's joy on regaining the coast of Italy after a short voyage; to Paul the Apostle's shipwreck near Malta; to Pisgah, Moses' mountain; and to the plight of the Israelites in Egypt. Sara Kemble Knight compares herself to Lot's wife during a canoe ride in which she was afraid to look around for fear of tipping the frail craft. She also refers to Cynthia, the Greek goddess of the moon, and to the Nereidees, who were Greek nymphs. There is also a reference to the prophet Balaam's talking donkey. Benjamin Franklin alludes to the Greek ideas of Socrates and Pythagoras in his essay on moral perfection, and Anne Bradstreet's title *The Tenth Muse Lately Sprung up in America* is a reference to the nine Greek Muses. William Byrd alludes to one of Aesop's fables and to one of Chaucer's *Canterbury Tales.* Phyllis Wheatley alludes to the legend of Damon and Pythias, the Roman goddess Aurora, and to "Celestial Salem" (Heaven).

1-16. Vocabulary List

1-17. Squanto's Turkey

The list contains words found in commonly read colonial literature. The spelling and vocabulary exercises use many of them. Several of the words are also on the list approved for study for the SAT/PSAT test.

1-18. A Borrower Be

This is the first of several exercises that look at etymology. A basic research tool—the dictionary—and a fairly quick look at etymology and language growth are introduced. Other worksheets will add to this beginning.

1-19. Think It Through

Thinking skills required to do this worksheet are the same as those needed to achieve on the English sections of standardized tests such as the SAT/PSAT. More important, however, students need these skills to become mature, independent, and original thinkers. Worksheets in other chapters also address these skills. The answers for the last exercise follow.

Answers

Analogies	Synonyms	Antonyms
1. B (part of plant harvested)	1. A	C
2. D (location)	2. D	B
3. A (modern vs. ancient)	3. B	C
4. E (top of each)		

PROJECT IDEAS

Teach a Class

Elementary students love to have help from high school students. A group of students go to a nearby elementary school and teach a subject from colonial literature. Perhaps they can show the youngsters what it was like to cross the Atlantic Ocean on the Mayflower. Any other colonial event would do as well. The students should plan audiovisual aids carefully and have some activities in which the elementary students could participate. An original skit could make up part of the lesson/program.

Map Activity

Enlarge a map of the United States to wall size (you can do this with an overhead projector). As the literature of the United States is read, students can fill in locations, dates, and names of people and events in the proper geographic location. Colored markers can serve to code different eras or classifications. Students will see the march of "civilization" westward as well as the incursions from other areas. This same procedure can be followed with a time line using the items in the chronology that follows, as well as information from other sources.

Preach a Sermon

A student or several students write a "typical" Puritan sermon directed to people today. One of the students preaches the sermon much as it would have been done then.

Build a Colony

A group of students construct to scale any typical colonial-era building or dwelling. Others could collect recipes or pictures of typical clothing. Original drawings would be even more effective.

Research

Research the following: colonial music or art, colonial teenagers and their activities, education for this period, tools and utensils used in everyday life, or many other topics the students could suggest. Many of the worksheets can be used as the basis for further research or for an oral report to the class.

Debate

Settler vs. native American: My way represents the better way to live in this land.

CHRONOLOGY

c. 35,000–8,000 B.C. Earliest native American settlements in the future United States

1492—Columbus reached the New World

1513—Ponce de Leon lands in Florida

Balboa discovers the Pacific Ocean on September 25

1519—Magellan circumnavigates the globe

1528—Cabeza de Vaca reaches Florida

1540—de Cardenas discovers the Grand Canyon

1541—De Soto reaches the Mississippi River

1542—Cabeza de Vaca, *The Shipwrecked Men*

1565—St. Augustine, Florida, is founded by the Spanish

1603—Elizabeth I dies; James becomes king

1607—Jamestown, Virginia, is founded

1608—John Smith, *A True Relation of Virginia*

1609—Santa Fe, New Mexico, is founded

1620—The Mayflower Compact

Plymouth, Massachusetts, is settled

1624—John Smith, *The General History*

1625—James I dies; Charles becomes king

1630—Salem, Massachusetts, the Massachusetts Bay Colony, is established

1635—Boston Latin School, the first public school in America, is founded

1636—Harvard University, the first college in America, is founded

1639—Cambridge, Massachusetts, has the first printing press in America

1649—Charles I is beheaded; Puritans under Cromwell reign

1650—Anne Bradstreet, *The Tenth Muse Lately Sprung Up in America*

1660—Charles II becomes king

1663—Cotton Mather in born

1670—Charleston is founded

1673—Joliet and Marquette explore the upper Mississippi River

1682—Mary Rowlandson writes of her captivity among the Indians

1683—The *New England Primer,* the primary textbook to be used for two centuries, is published

1692—Martha Carrier is executed for witchcraft

1704—Boston *News-Letter,* the first newspaper in America, is put into circulation

Sarah Kemble Knight, *Journal*

1718—New Orleans is founded

1723—Benjamin Franklin arrives in Philadelphia

1729—Baltimore is founded

1730—Benjamin Franklin, *Poore Richard's Almanack*

1739—"The Great Awakening" begins

1741—Jonathan Edwards, "Sinners in the Hands of an Angry God"

1752—Benjamin Franklin discovers that lightning is electricity

1755-1763—French and Indian War

BIBLIOGRAPHY

Further Reading for Students and Teachers

Armstrong, Virginia Irving, ed. *I Have Spoken: American History Through the Voices of the Indians.* Athens: Ohio University Press, 1971.

Austin, Jane. *David Alden's Daughter and Other Stories of Colonial Times.* Short Story Index Reprint Series. Salem, NH: Ayer, 1892.

Dorson, Richard M., ed. *America Begins: Early American Writings.* New York: Fawcett, 1966.

Dutton, Bertha P. *American Indians of the Southwest.* Albuquerque: University of New Mexico Press, 1985.

Hart, J. D. *Oxford Companion to American Literature.* New York: Oxford University Press, 1983.

Hodge, Frederick W., and Theodore H. Lewis, eds. *Spanish Explorers in the Southern United States, 1528–1543.* New York: Scribner's, 1959.

Holliday, Carl. *Woman's Life in Colonial Days.* Williamstown, MA: Corner House, 1959.

Karleson, Carl F. *The Devil in the Shape of a Woman: Witchcraft in Colonial New England.* New York: Norton, 1987.

Marriott, Alice, and Carol K. Rachlin. *Plains Indians Mythology.* New York: New American Library, 1985.

Miller, Arthur. *The Crucible.* New York: Penguin, 1976.

Morison, Samuel Eliot. *The European Discovery of America.* New York: Oxford University Press, 1971.

Nash, Gary B. *Red, White, and Black: The Peoples of Early America.* Englewood Cliffs, NJ: Prentice Hall, 1982.

Parker, Rodger D. *Wellsprings of a Nation: America Before 1801.* Worcester, MA: American Antiquarian, 1977.

Porter, Donald C. *White Indian.* New York: Bantam, 1984.

Roberts, Elizabeth Madox. *The Great Meadow.* Saint Simons Island, GA: Mockingbird Books, 1975.

Schlesinger, Arthur M., Jr., *The Birth of a Nation: A Portrait of the American People in the Eve of Independence.* Boston: Houghton Mifflin, 1988.

Stratton, Eugene A. *Plymouth Colony: Its History and People, 1620–1691.* Salt Lake City, UT: Ancestry, 1987.

Wright, Louis B. *The Atlantic Frontier: Colonial American Civilization, 1607–1763.* Des Plaines, IL: Greenwood, 1980.

Name ______________________________ Date ______________

1-1. IT HAPPENED WHERE?

Map Skills / Seeing Relationships

DIRECTIONS: As you read literature from the colonial period, fill in the map shown here. Include names, events, and people, as well as locations. Using a different color for each, color lightly the New England, middle, and southern colonies. You may number each map entry and fill in the material beside the map.

Name ______________________________ Date ______________

1-2. A WHOLE LAND BEYOND

DIRECTIONS: Life was going on in other parts of the country (1492–1760). Expand your horizons and note some of these events and areas. Fill in the map below with as many events, names, and locations as you can and watch as settlement moves westward. Note Indian nations, Spanish and French settlements, and any others you can remember.

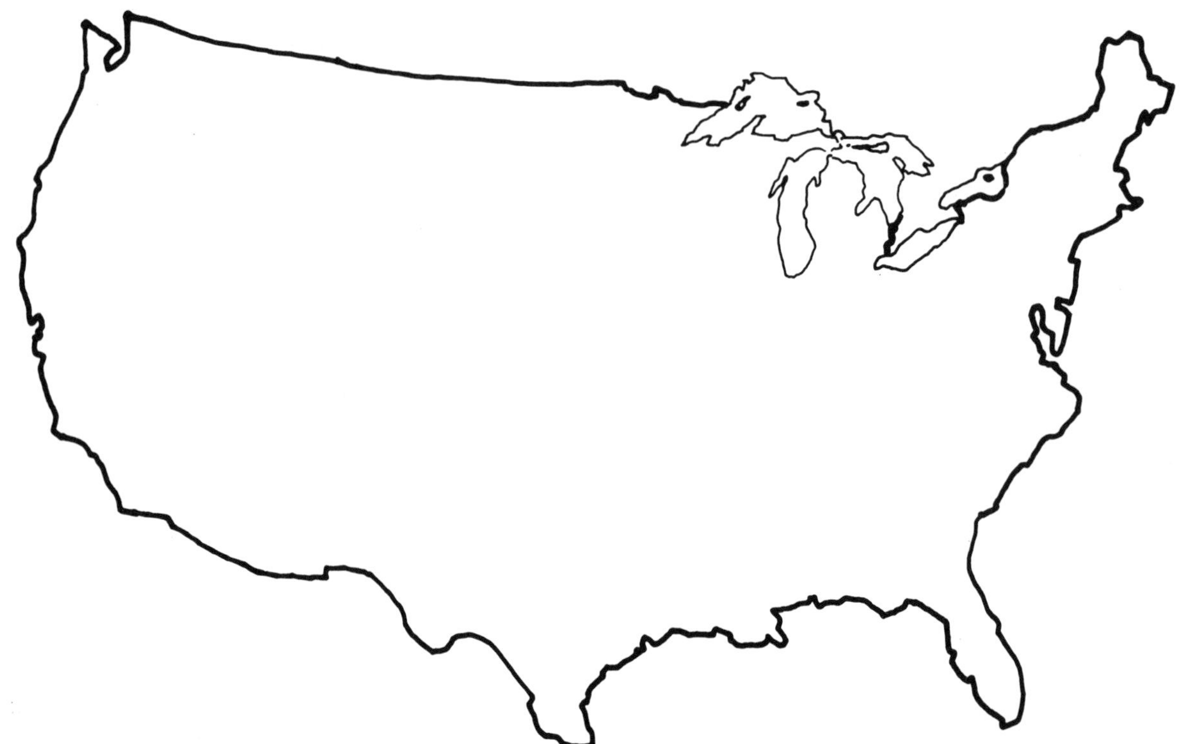

Name ______________________________ Date ______________

1-3. TO GO—OR NOT TO GO

You are a Pilgrim living in England in the early 1600s. You do not feel free to practice your religion as you would like. There is room for one more person on the Mayflower. Should you leave your native land forever to live in a new and unknown land? To go or not to go—what do you do?

List the reasons for going and for staying. Then make your decision.

TO GO	or	NOT TO GO
1. ______________________		1. ______________________
______________________		______________________
2. ______________________		2. ______________________
______________________		______________________
3. ______________________		3. ______________________
______________________		______________________
4. ______________________		4. ______________________
______________________		______________________
5. ______________________		5. ______________________
______________________		______________________
6. ______________________		6. ______________________
______________________		______________________
7. ______________________		7. ______________________
______________________		______________________
8. ______________________		8. ______________________
______________________		______________________

DECISION (circle one): GO STAY

Name ______________________ Date ____________

1-4. MAYFLOWER MOVING

You are a young Pilgrim who, along with your wife and daughter, is about to embark on the Mayflower for the New Land. What will you pack to take with you? What will you leave behind?

PACK	LEAVE
____________________	____________________
____________________	____________________
____________________	____________________
____________________	____________________
____________________	____________________
____________________	____________________
____________________	____________________
____________________	____________________
____________________	____________________
____________________	____________________
____________________	____________________
____________________	____________________
____________________	____________________
____________________	____________________

Name ______________________ Date ____________

1-5. A DAY IN THE LIFE

Women in the colonies were active, aware partners in the settlement of the New World. Many of them left literature in the form of letters, diaries, journals, poems, and narratives. Women like Anne Bradstreet, Sarah Kemble Knight, Mary Rowlandson, Eliza Pickney, Abigail Adams, Margaret Winthrop, and Mrs. Benjamin Franklin have all left written information about their lives and times.

DIRECTIONS: Using the chart below, fill in the activities that could have made up a typical day for a colonial woman.

HOUR ______________________

A.M. ______________________

7–8 ______________________

8–9 ______________________

9–10 ______________________

10–11 ______________________

11–12 ______________________

P.M. ______________________

12–1 ______________________

1–2 ______________________

2–3 ______________________

3–4 ______________________

4–5 ______________________

5–6 ______________________

6–7 ______________________

7–8 ______________________

8–9 ______________________

9–10 ______________________

10–11 ______________________

11–12 ______________________

Name ______________________________ Date ______________

1-6. THE PROMISE AND THE REALITY

The Meaning of America

In diaries, sermons, historical accounts, speeches, stories, and poems the immigrant men and women of all areas expressed what they found in the New Land and their hopes for the future. These included dreams for the nation as well as personal and spiritual dreams. They foresaw a New Land built on these dreams.

DIRECTIONS: List some of the dreams and plans our immigrant founders had for the New Land. Then look at the United States today and decide if we have the country they envisioned. List the author of each vision.

1. Author ______________________________ Vision ______________

____

____

Today ____

2. Author ______________________________ Vision ______________

____

____

Today ____

3. Author ______________________________ Vision ______________

____

____

Today ____

4. Author ______________________________ Vision ______________

____

____

Today ____

5. Author ______________________________ Vision ______________

____

____

Today ____

Name ______________________________ Date ____________

1-7. THEN AND NOW

From the beginning, the country that would become the United States had a rich and varied culture. The thirty-thousand-year-old native American culture was one of beauty and depth. In the sixteenth and seventeenth centuries many cultures began to meet. They either "melted" together or clashed. Large numbers of Spanish, British, French, Dutch, Swedes, Germans, and Africans, among others, arrived.

1. Think of two incidents in which two cultures met and clashed.

____

____

2. Think of two incidents in which cultures met and "melted" together peacefully.

____

____

3. Choose one of the incidents from each of the two preceding entries and explain how the outcomes of these incidents can still be seen in the United States today.

____

____

____

____

____

____

4. Are there places in the United States today where pockets of the seven cultural groups named above can still be found? Name three or four.

____

____

____

____

Name ______________________________ Date ______________

1-8. A ROUSING SERMON

Choose a sermon by one of the great colonial preachers. After reading it, describe in two or three paragraphs the average member of that preacher's congregation. For example, what were his or her religious beliefs, how did these beliefs affect daily life, what would be major sins, what was the punishment for sin?

Name ______________________________ Date ______________

1-9. NORTH AND SOUTH

As the colonies developed into a nation, differences between the North and the South became more apparent, culminating in the Civil War. Even though early settlers had much in common, were any of these differences evident from the very beginning? As you read the literature of the colonial period, note the similarities of Plymouth and Jamestown. Then note the differences. List four of each below.

	SIMILAR	DIFFERENT
1.	______________	______________
2.	______________	______________
3.	______________	______________
4.	______________	______________

Using these ideas as an informal outline, expand them into a three-paragraph essay. The first two paragraphs will contain the ideas you listed above; the third will be your brief conclusion about whether the seeds of the Civil War were already planted in these early days of our country. Begin your rough draft below and continue it on the back of the paper. (Write your final draft on another sheet of paper and attach it.)

Name ______________________________ Date ______________

1-10. THE BEST THINGS IN LIFE

DIRECTIONS: You have lived in the colonies for one year now and believe your new life to be the only way to live. Write a friendly letter to a friend back home telling about the place you now live and trying to persuade him or her to join you.

Dear ____________________,

Name ______________________________ Date ______________

1-11. THEY SAID IT THEIR WAY

DIRECTIONS: Copy two descriptions or attitudes regarding nature, one by a European settler and one by a native American. Then do the exercises below.

Colonial author ______________________________

____

____

____

Native American author ______________________________

____

____

____

1. Is the description more like prose or poetry?

2. What was the settlers' attitude toward nature? What was the Native Americans' attitude toward nature?

3. Look at the words each group uses. Describe the word choices.

4. Look at the sentences in each. Write a one-sentence description of the sentences used.

5. Using the conclusions you formed above, write a short essay comparing or contrasting the attitudes toward nature and the writing styles you have observed.

Name ______________________________ Date ______________

1-12. RHYME TIME

Rhyme Scheme

Rhyme is present when the end sound of one word is the same as that of another word. For example, the words *dock* and *clock* rhyme. Therefore, the following two lines are said to rhyme:

Hickory Dickory Dock
The mouse ran up the clock

A poet will add meaning and order to his or her poetry by arranging those rhyming lines into a pattern called a *rhyme scheme.* This creates a pleasant musical effect. Rhyme is also related to meaning, for it brings two or more words sharply together. You can determine the rhyme scheme of a poem by assigning letters to the end words. Assign a different letter in alphabetical order to each new rhyme. For example, the rhyme scheme of the following stanza is aabb:

If ever two were one, then surely we. a
If ever man were loved by wife, then thee; a
If ever wife was happy in a man, b
Compare with me, ye women, if you can. b
(Anne Bradstreet)

Copy two stanzas from a poem written during colonial times and write the rhyme scheme. Did the author of the poem intend the poem to be humorous or serious? Following the poem, write how the rhyme scheme might have contributed to the meaning.

____

____

____

____

____

____

____

____

____

____

____

____

Name ______________________ Date ______________

1-13. IT'S A WHAT?!?

Metaphors and Similes

A *metaphor* is a figure of speech that makes an implied comparison between two things that are essentially unlike each other. For example, "The fog came in on little cat feet" implies a comparison between the action of fog with that of a cat.

DIRECTIONS: Copy two metaphors from colonial literature and tell what two things are being compared.

1. ______________________________

____

2. ______________________________

____

Now, write an original metaphor describing a bright, warm October day.

____

A *simile* is a figure of speech that makes a direct comparison between two things that are essentially unlike each other. The words *like, as,* or *than* almost always appear in the comparison. For example, "He is as strong as a bull" compares the strength of a man with that of a bull.

DIRECTIONS: Copy two similes from colonial literature and tell what two things are being compared in each.

1. ______________________________

____

2. ______________________________

____

Now, write an original simile describing a young, prancing colt.

____

Name ______________________________ Date ______________

1-14. WORTH A THOUSAND WORDS

Allusions

An *allusion* is a reference to an incident, character, or location in another well-known work (literature, art, music, a famous speech, or movie). The new work may be greatly enhanced in depth of meaning by incorporating the ideas and feelings of the original work. For example, by calling a long journey an *odyssey,* Odysseus' trying and adventurous trip home following the Trojan War is brought to mind. Although the works of Homer are alluded to often, perhaps the grand champion source of allusions from literature is the Bible.

DIRECTIONS: Find three allusions in colonial literature and explain the reference. Then try your hand at writing one. Describe a situation or incident, using an allusion in the description.

Allusion 1 ______________________________

____

____

Allusion 2 ______________________________

____

____

Allusion 3 ______________________________

____

____

My allusion ______________________________

____

____

What did the allusion add to your literary situation?

____

____

____

____

Name ______________________________ Date ______________

1-15. ONOMATOPOEIA

Poetry often makes use of *onomatopoeia* to help create a sound. This is especially true of native American poetry, which was often chanted or sung and accompanied by dancing.

Onomatopoeia is the use of words whose sound indicates their meaning. For example, *plop, slurp, buzz, tick-tock,* and *cuckoo* are onomatopoetic words. A *slurp* sounds like the thing it describes or names. These sound words add much to a poem's meaning.

1. Find two examples of onomatopoeia in colonial poetry and list the source.

   a. ______________________________

   ____

   Source ______________________________

   b. ______________________________

   ____

   Source ______________________________

2. Now, make up two examples of onomatopoeia of your own to describe water.

   a. ______________________________

   ____

   b. ______________________________

   ____

3. Next, form these sounds and images into your own short poem.

   ____

   ____

   ____

   ____

   ____

   ____

   ____

1-16. VOCABULARY LIST

1. adversity
2. aristocrat
3. arrow
4. ashore
5. asunder
6. avail
7. beauty
8. bog
9. brethren
10. canoe
11. celestial
12. chaff
13. chide
14. chipmunk
15. colony
16. comprise
17. crisis
18. crops
19. crossbow
20. divers
21. divine (noun)
22. eagle
23. emaciate
24. feast
25. firefly
26. freedom
27. harbor
28. hurricane
29. impious
30. inalienable
31. Indians
32. indolent
33. journey
34. lamentable
35. laws
36. loathsome
37. maize
38. manifold
39. moccasin
40. mortal
41. mountain
42. omnipotent
43. persevere
44. Pilgrim
45. piteous
46. plantation
47. prodigal
48. profane
49. prudence
50. Puritan
51. quagmire
52. raccoon
53. recompense
54. repine
55. rights
56. sagacious
57. sermon
58. smite
59. squash
60. staunch
61. succor
62. sundry
63. swamp
64. tadpole
65. tobacco
66. toleration
67. traverse
68. turkey
69. tyranny
70. unwieldy
71. warp
72. weft
73. wigwam
74. witch
75. witness

Name ______________________________ Date ______________

1-17. SQUANTO'S TURKEY

DIRECTIONS: Get that turkey! Begin at the *upper left-hand corner* and draw a continuous line from one correctly spelled word to the next. You may move horizontally and vertically, but do not move diagonally. Time yourself. Good luck!

Pilgrim	jurney	wagwim	mortle	inalienable	prodigal	crops
beauty	repine	herricane	asunder	prudence	devine	manifold
mountin	indolent	chipmonk	impious	lawz	persevere	moccasin
eagle	divers	lamantable	staunch	advercety	weft	worp
emaciate	crosbow	tiranny	TURKEY!	freedum	smite	unwieldy
rights	arrow	canoo	profanne	achore	krisis	squash
quakmire	chaff	puritin	tolerasion	plantation	Indians	journey
feest	omnipotent	brethren	tobaco	sermon	aristacrat	harber
colany	rakoon	swamp	sundry	traverse	wicth	sajaceous

Name ______________________________ Date ______________

1-18. A BORROWER BE

Etymology

A dictionary gives not only the meaning of a word but also its history. This is called the *etymology* of that word. By checking the material in brackets after a dictionary entry, you can get a brief review of the word's historical development. For example, the word *etymology* itself came into English from Old French, which got it from the Latin language, which got it from the Greek language.

Look up the etymologies of the following words:

1. canoe
2. hurricane
3. raccoon
4. tobacco
5. skunk
6. hominy
7. Mackinaw
8. Massachusetts

In two or three sentences, draw a conclusion about why British English and American English have become so different.

____

____

____

____

In two or three sentences, draw a conclusion about the development of languages in general.

____

____

____

____

____

____

Name ______________________________ Date ______________

1-19. THINK IT THROUGH

Analogies test your reasoning ability as well as your knowledge of vocabulary. Analogies demonstrate a way of thinking that allows you to see parallel relationships. Complete the analogies below by circling the correct answer.

Example: Cat: Fur ::
A. Wing : Arm C. Bird : Feathers
B. Ground : Air D. Paw : Foot E. Mouse : Worm
Read the analogy as follows: *Cat is to fur as bird is to feathers.* Translation: Cats are covered by fur; birds are covered by feathers. The answer is C.

1. Tobacco : Leaf : :
   A. Crops : Market
   B. Coffee : Bean
   C. North : South
   D. Raccoon : Animal
   E. Can : Container
2. Ocean : Typhoon : :
   A. Ship : Sail
   B. Field : Plot
   C. East : West
   D. Prairie : Tornado
   E. Country : City
3. Clock : Rifle : :
   A. Hourglass : Arrow
   B. Time : Mainspring
   C. Direction : Map
   D. Bullet : Lead
   E. Deer : Game
4. Peak : Mountain : :
   A. Sun : Earth
   B. Grass : Green
   C. Forest : Woods
   D. Money : Wallet
   E. Crest : Wave

Synonyms and Antonyms

A synonym is a word that means the same or nearly the same as another word. Antonyms are words that are opposite in meaning. You will find a synonym and an antonym answer for each word below. Mark the synonyms with an S and the antonyms with an A.

1. Staunch
   A. Steadfast B. Leaky C. Wavering D. Damp E. Seaworthy
2. Tyranny
   A. Napoleon B. Democracy C. Monarch D. Dictatorship E. Elizabeth
3. Mortal
   A. Sinful B. Temporary C. Eternal D. Mankind E. God

Section 2
THE REVOLUTION

1760-1800 Franklin to Paine

SKILLS INDEX

Literary Skills		Worksheet
Author's purpose	2–12	Poetry to Prose
Fiction, novel, short story, play	2–14	Oh, Really !?!
Heroic couplet, iambic pentameter, meter	2–16	Heroic Couplet
Nonfiction, essay, biography, autobiography	2–15	The Truth, the Whole Truth . . .

Writing Skills		Worksheet
Aphorisms	2–13	A Penny Saved . . .
Comparison and contrast	2–8	The American Dream
	2–10	Divinely Guided
	2–2	Puritanism Continues
	2–4	Rebellion vs. Loyalty
Exposition	2–3	The Idea of Freedom
	2–2	Puritanism Continues
Narration	2–9	Martha
	2–19	Westward
News reporting	2–6	The Five W's
Parallelism, rhetorical question, repetition	2–11	Say It Again, Pat
Paraphrasing	2–12	Poetry to Prose
Persuasion	2–4	Rebellion vs. Loyalty

Thinking Skills		Worksheet
Analysis	2–12	Poetry to Prose
	2–7	Politics of the Revolution
Drawing Conclusions	2–10	Divinely Guided
	2–4	Rebellion vs. Loyalty
	2–1	What Do You Do?
Generalizing	2–8	The American Dream
	2–13	A Penny Saved . . .
	2–10	Divinely Guided
	2–9	Martha
	2–1	What Do You Do?
	2–5	What's in a Name?

Vocabulary Skills		Worksheet
Analogies, synonyms, antonyms	2–20	Think It Through
Archaic words and usages	2–19	Westward
Prefixes	2–18	Beginnings
Vocabulary list	2–17	75 Words

Other Skills		Worksheet
Cartoon drawing	2–7	Politics of the Revolution
Map reading	2–5	What's in a Name?
News media	2–8	The American Dream

WORKSHEET NOTES

2-1. What Do You Do?

In this exercise students use their knowledge of history and literature to recall the occupations of well-known people of this era. Then they are to generalize and to draw conclusions from their list of occupations. A bit of role playing could help here.

2-2. Puritanism Continues

Building on writing skills begun in Section 1, students write a five-paragraph expository composition. Again, the comparison and contrast technique is emphasized. There can be some flexibility in the thesis statement.

2-3. The Idea of Freedom

Contrary to what some people would like to believe, freedom is not the right to do what you want when you want. Freedom, as it relates to the growth of the United States, often meant something very specific, at least to three of our founders. Students will work with this idea while they hone their skills in the writing of thesis statements. It often seems that once the thesis statement is worked out, putting together the composition is fairly simple.

2-4. Rebellion vs. Loyalty

Declaring independence from England was an extraordinarily courageous act. The reasons for doing so were based on principles for which men and women were ready to sacrifice everything, even their lives. England was the leading naval and military power of the era. How could a ragtag group of colonists with no central government or army possibly defeat her? Also, the colonies needed England's manufactured products. Even more daunting to many was that they would no longer be English. Many people, despite the difficulties, felt loyalty to, pride in, and love for their "mother" country. As the students do this exercise, perhaps they will develop an understanding of the difficulty of this choice.

2-5. What's in a Name?

Students will use their map-reading and generalizing skills to do this exercise. When the English settled on the East Coast, they often brought part of home with them in the form of geographical names. In the northern colonies we often see names such as New York, Cambridge, Waterbury, New Haven, New Hampshire, Pittsburgh, Pennsylvania, New Jersey, and Roxbury. In the South, some of the early place names are Virginia, Georgia, Carolina, Jamestown, Charleston, Williamsburg, Maryland, Raleigh, Georgetown, and the James River. Students should see a pattern begin to emerge. People in the colonies recognized the "mother" country. It becomes obvious, however, that people in the North remembered home and people who stood for a principle, whereas people in the South remembered home and the monarchy. Logically, it would have been much more difficult for the South to take up arms against England. Of course, native American names will be found in all areas.

2-6. The Five W's

Students will need their knowledge of news writing and of the literature and history of the era to do this exercise. They will also need to do some role playing. They will see that in writing the first paragraph of a news article, every word counts. Any word that does not directly add to the information required by the five W's should not be there.

2-7. Politics of the Revolution

Drawing a political caricature or cartoon allows students to look closely at and analyze an event or person from a new point of view. Students will see that today's political cartoons have a long history.

2-8. The American Dream

This exercise requires students to use today's news media to compare and contrast ideals of the revolutionary era with those of the present time. Once again, they will see that what was written and spoken then does matter today.

2-9. Martha

Role playing helps people and events come to life in the minds of students. What was life like at home while the war was being fought? Did Martha perhaps have doubts about owning slaves while George was off fighting for freedom? What were the everyday chores that kept a plantation operational? What was it like to fear for the lives of those close to you?

2-10. Divinely Guided

This exercise is one of several throughout the book that traces the idea that the United States has had a history based to a great extent on religious principles. This idea can be traced through all of the literary periods of the past three hundred years. For example, Patrick Henry in his famous speech referred to responsibility to "God and country" as though it were one and the same. In the Declaration, Jefferson referred to "nature's God" entitling the colonies to "separate and equal station" and the Creator's endowment of mankind with certain "inalienable rights." Today we pledge allegiance to "one nation, under God," and open each new session of Congress with a prayer for divine guidance.

2-11. Say It Again, Pat

Three common speaking/writing devices are highlighted in this exercise. It is essential to good writing and to the understanding of style that students be familiar with them.

2-12. Poetry to Prose

To read, understand, analyze for author's purpose, and paraphrase a poem requires some fairly mature literary skills, skills that grow with practice. Sharing these paragraphs with the class should be interesting. An insight into the thinking of others can help widen point of view.

2-13. A Penny Saved . . .

Aphorisms, it seems, are always with us. And they do usually reflect the basic values of a society. It should be interesting to note whether the students' aphorisms are specific to time and location or are generally relevant.

2-14. Oh, Really!?!

2-15. The Truth, the Whole Truth . . .

2-16. Heroic Couplet

Using literature of the revolutionary era, these three exercises review several basic literary terms. The first two present the ideas of *fiction* and *nonfiction* in a very basic format. The third is more challenging and requires the understanding of several fairly advanced poetic skills.

2-17. Vocabulary List

2-18. Beginnings

2-19. Westward

2-20. Think It Through

Once again, the vocabulary section begins with a list of words from literature of the period. The three vocabulary exercises are based on this list, which can be used for any number of exercises such as spelling tests, and sentence and paragraph writing. The first exercise uses the list to help students understand basic prefixes; the second is a writing assignment dealing with the idea of archaic words and usages. "Think It Through" is to help students work with analogies, synonyms, and antonyms. The answers for the last exercise follow.

Answers:

Analogies	Synonyms	Antonyms
1. D	1. C	B
2. B	2. C	A
3. C	3. E	D
4. A	4. B	C
5. B	5. A	E
6. A		

PROJECT IDEAS

Class Newspaper

Publish a revolutionary-era newspaper. Establish a location and date. Have the usual sections: news, editorials, entertainment, society, advice, frontier news, sports, classified, comics. The class can be divided into groups for this project. Work on the newspaper can be shared with the American history classes.

Give a Speech

Two students give rousing, street-corner speeches, one urging the colonies to remain with the "mother" country, the other pleading the cause of independence. Have the speakers designate the time, location, and audience type. The listeners then react accordingly.

Propaganda

Two or three students define common propaganda techniques and then decide if any were used by revolutionary-era writers and speakers.

Plan a Trip

Boston's AAA must plan a trip to Savannah, Georgia, for the summer of 1770 for a client. Plan his or her trip: Include a map, overnight accommodations, methods of travel, miles to be covered per day, and possible delays along the way. Would a side trip to Florida be advisable at this time?

Research

Research the following: Monticello, Mt. Vernon, Franklin as a scientist, pubs, the Spanish presence on the continent, a woman's life, an average family dwelling, conflicts with native Americans, the theater, black literature, teenagers' music, or the exploration of the frontier. Once again, these projects can be shared with the class as oral reports.

Budget Your Income

A student can research the average earnings of a laborer and the cost of the necessities of life. Devise a family for this laborer and budget his income accordingly. A modern-day budget form can be used.

CHRONOLOGY

1762—Printing press set up in Georgia

1764—Otis, *Rights of the British Colonies*

1765—Watt invents the steam engine

Sons of Liberty formed

1766—Queens College (Rutgers) founded

1767—Godfrey, *The Prince of Parthia*, first produced American play

The Psalms of David, first music book printed in the colonies

1767-1768—Daniel Boone explores Kentucky

1770—The Boston Massacre

1773—Tea Act

The Boston Tea Party

P. Wheatley, *Poems*

First theater established in Charleston, South Carolina

1774—First Continential Congress meets in Philadelphia

Jefferson, *Summary of View of Rights of British America*

Rush, *Natural History of Medicine Among Indians of North America*

1775-1783—Revolutionary War

1775—Paul Revere rides

Battles of Bunker Hill, Lexington, and Concord

Mrs. Warren, *The Group*

Patrick Henry's speech in Virginia

Second Continental Congress meets in Philadelphia

Washington becomes head of the Continental forces

The postal system is established

1776—Jefferson, The Declaration of Independence

Paine, *Common Sense*

Congress votes for independence, July 2 (12-0)

Declaration is approved, July 4

Washington defeats the Hessians

1777—Stars and Stripes named national flag by Congress

Burgoyne surrenders

1778—Treaty with France

Franklin, *Ephemera*

Freneau, *American Independence*

1780—Treason of Benedict Arnold

American Academy of Arts and Sciences founded

1781—Articles of Confederation ratified

Cornwallis surrenders to Washington at Yorktown

Hopkinson, *The Temple of Minerva,* first grand opera

1782—Peace talks begin in Paris

De Crèvecoeur, *Letters from an American Farmer*

First American museum is established in Philadelphia

1783—Articles of Peace ratified

N. Webster, *The American Spelling Book*

Washington Irving is born

1784—New York City named the capital of the country

1786—Freneau, *Poems*

1787—Constitutional Convention opens

Tyler, *The Contrast,* first American comedy

1788—Ratification of the Constitution

1789—Washington wins first presidential election

The French Revolution begins

The Power of Sympathy, first American novel by William Hill Brown

The federal government is established

1790—Benjamin Franklin dies

Industrial Revolution begins

Southwest Territory organized

1791—Paine, *Rights of Man*

Vermont admitted to the Union

1792—Kentucky admitted to the Union

Washington wins a second term

1793—Whitney invents the cotton gin

1796—Washington's Farewell Address; Adams is president

1799—Washington dies

1800—Library of Congress founded

Washington, D.C., becomes capital of country

Weems, *Life of Washington*

BIBLIOGRAPHY

Further Reading for Students and Teachers

Alden, John R. *A History of the American Revolution.* Abilene, TX: Quality Paperbacks, 1989.

Cunningham, Noble E. *In Pursuit of Reason: The Life of Thomas Jefferson.* Baton Rouge: Louisiana State University Press, 1987.

Ellet, Elizabeth. *The Women of the American Revolution.* Williamstown, MA: Corner House, 1980.

Flexner, James Thomas. *Washington: The Indispensable Man.* Boston: Little, Brown, 1974.

———. *The Young Hamilton.* Boston: Little, Brown, 1978.

Forbes, Esther. *Paul Revere and the World He Lived In.* Boston: Houghton Mifflin, 1962.

Franklin, Benjamin. *Writings.* New York: Viking, 1987.

Morris, Richard B. *The American Revolution: A Short History.* Melbourne, FL: Krieger, 1979.

Portell-Vila, Herminio. *Los Otros Extranjeros en la Revolucion Norteamericana.* Miami Ediciones, 1978.

Rankin, Hugh F. *The Theater in Colonial America.* Chapel Hill: University of North Carolina Press, 1965.

Rossiter, Clinton. *Seventeen Eighty-seven: The Grand Convention.* New York: Norton, 1987.

Schlesinger, Arthur M., Jr. *The Birth of a Nation: A Portrait of the American People on the Eve of Independence.* Boston: Houghton Mifflin, 1988.

Smith, Page. *A New Age Now Begins: A People's History of the American Revolution.* New York: Penguin, 1989.

Van Doren, Carl C. *Benjamin Franklin.* Des Plaines, IL: Greenwood, 1973.

VanEvery, Dale. *A Company of Heroes: The American Frontier, 1775-1783.* New York: Morrow, 1989.

Van Wyck, Mason F. *Wild Horizon.* Boston: Little, Brown, 1966.

Name ______________________________ Date ______________

2-1. WHAT DO YOU DO?

The types of jobs that prevail in a society tell us much about the times. List twelve people that lived during the revolutionary period and tell how they earned a living.

	PERSON	OCCUPATION
1.	______________	______________
2.	______________	______________
3.	______________	______________
4.	______________	______________
5.	______________	______________
6.	______________	______________
7.	______________	______________
8.	______________	______________
9.	______________	______________
10.	______________	______________
11.	______________	______________
12.	______________	______________

Drawing conclusions:

1. Based on the occupations you have just listed, can you make a list of the basic needs of people during this era?

2. Based on your list of occupations, what might be the position of women in this society?

Name ______________________________ Date ________________

2-2. PURITANISM CONTINUES

Even though the Puritan religion declined in importance at this time, did the ideas retain a place in our national character? To decide, choose a major Puritan thinker, such as Edwards, and a major thinker of the revolutionary era, such as Franklin. Write an essay comparing the two in the following areas: interests, writing style, and spiritual beliefs. Use as your thesis statement the idea that these people represent two aspects of the American personality. Use this page for your notes. Write the final draft on another sheet and attach it to this one.

Paragraph 1—thesis statement (2–3 sentences)

Paragraph 2—interests (6–8 sentences)

Paragraph 3—writing style (6–8 sentences)

Paragraph 4—spiritual beliefs or activities (6–8 sentences)

Paragraph 5—conclusion (2–3 sentences reiterating your now-proven thesis)

Name ______________________ Date ____________

2-3. THE IDEA OF FREEDOM

From its beginning, the United States has been identified with freedom. However, during the years from 1760 to 1800, freedom meant slightly different things to different people. In a thesis statement of two to three sentences, tell what freedom meant to the following authors.

Benjamin Franklin ______________________

____

____

____

____

Thomas Jefferson ______________________

____

____

____

____

Thomas Paine ______________________

____

____

____

____

Now, in a similar thesis statement, tell what freedom brings to mind for you.

____

____

____

Name ______________________________ Date ______________

2-4. REBELLION VS. LOYALTY

Many arguments were used to persuade the colonists to declare the nation's independence from England. List three authors of the revolutionary era who favored independence, then list their basic argument.

Author 1 ______________________________

Argument ______________________________

____

____

____

Author 2 ______________________________

Argument ______________________________

____

____

____

Author 3 ______________________________

Argument ______________________________

____

____

____

List at least four reasons why it was unwise to rebel against England at this time.

1. ______________________________
2. ______________________________
3. ______________________________
4. ______________________________

Name ______________________________ Date ______________

2-5. WHAT'S IN A NAME?

We can reap a wealth of information from names on a map. Look at a map of the East Coast of the United States. Starting in Maine and going south to Florida, notice the names of geographic locations: cities, counties, states, rivers, mountain ranges. Make a list of names below, arranging them according to northern and southern states. Then decide after whom or what these places were named.

NORTHERN LOCATIONS	NAMED FOR
1. ______________	______________
2. ______________	______________
3. ______________	______________
4. ______________	______________
5. ______________	______________

SOUTHERN LOCATIONS	NAMED FOR
1. ______________	______________
2. ______________	______________
3. ______________	______________
4. ______________	______________
5. ______________	______________

1. Can you read political loyalties in these names? For example, which areas would most likely remain loyal to England and the king?

2. Which areas would most hate being subjugated to England? Why?

3. Pretending you know nothing of American history, where would a rebellion most likely begin?

Name ______________________ Date ____________

2-6. THE FIVE W'S

Headlines were being made hourly during the revolutionary period. Choose three events that occurred at this time. Pretend you are a reporter covering the stories. Write a banner headline and the first paragraph of your stories. Remember, your lead paragraph must contain the five W's (who, what, when, where, why) and must be concisely written in one or two sentences.

Name of newspaper

Story 1 Headline ______________________

Paragraph ______________________

____

____

____

____

Story 2 Headline ______________________

Paragraph ______________________

____

____

____

____

Story 3 Headline ______________________

Paragraph ______________________

____

____

____

____

Name ______________________________ Date ______________

2-7. POLITICS OF THE REVOLUTION

Political cartoons and caricatures were prevalent during the revolutionary period, as they are now. One of the quickest ways to defeat an opposing person or view was, and is, to use ridicule. In the box below, draw a cartoon or caricature that may have appeared in a 1776 newspaper. Make certain that the subject is easily identifiable.

Name ______________________________ Date ______________

2-8. THE AMERICAN DREAM

Before and during the American Revolution this country founded its government on the idea that its citizens are entitled to "life, liberty and the pursuit of happiness." Are these ideas still relevant today, or have we outgrown them?

Be aware of the various news media this week—newspapers, television, radio, and news magazines—and list four areas in which the battles for "life, liberty and the pursuit of happiness" are still being fought. List the sources of your ideas.

1. ______________________________

____

____

Source (title, date) ______________________________

2. ______________________________

____

____

Source ______________________________

3. ______________________________

____

____

Source ______________________________

4. ______________________________

____

____

Source ______________________________

Can you list three "inalienable rights" we may have today that were not of concern to the founders of our government?

1. ______________________________

2. ______________________________

3. ______________________________

Name ______________________________ Date ______________

2-9. MARTHA

You are Mrs. George Washington. Your husband is off fighting a war, leaving you to run a Virginia plantation called Mt. Vernon. It is late, the end of a typical day. Before going to sleep you tell your diary about your day and your feelings concerning events. What do you write? Date your entry.

Dear Diary,

Name ______________________________ Date ______________

2-10. DIVINELY GUIDED

A "goodly" number of colonial-era writers and preachers felt that their country was divinely guided. God's hand was seen in everything. Religion during the Revolution was not quite so potent a part of daily life. Did the idea of divine guidance fall by the wayside or was it still an integral part of the founding of our government? Can you cite three examples from events, official documents, or products to show that this idea was still very much alive? Can you also cite three examples to show that this idea could still be alive today?

THEN 1. ______________________________

2. ______________________________

3. ______________________________

NOW 1. ______________________________

2. ______________________________

3. ______________________________

In your opinion, is all of this consistent with the "separation of church and state" as set forth in the Constitution? Explain your answer.

____

Name ______________________________ Date ______________

2-11. SAY IT AGAIN, PAT

Writers and speakers use various devices to emphasize their ideas, create unity, and involve the audience in the process. Three of the most common are listed here. Find two examples of each from the literature of the revolutionary period and identify the author.

Repetition—repeating sounds, words, phrases, or sentences for emphasis or effect, for example, "Pay me now, or pay me later."

Parallelism—wording a phrase or sentence so that two or more ideas are expressed in the same grammatical form, for example, "Ask not what your country can do for you; ask what you can do for your country."

Rhetorical question—a question to which no answer is expected, for example, "If winter comes, can spring be far behind?"

Repetition ______________________________

____

____

____

____

______________________________ Author ______________

Parallelism ______________________________

____

____

____

____

______________________________ Author ______________

Rhetorical question ______________________________

____

____

____

______________________________ Author ______________

Name ____________________ Date ____________

2-12. POETRY TO PROSE

For many people, reading, understanding, and enjoying a good poem is an extremely rewarding experience. The poets of this period of American history were breaking new ground in the areas of style and subject matter and were laying the groundwork for a truly American poetry.

DIRECTIONS: Choose a poem from your text and paraphrase in prose the first stanza. As you do this, you will begin to see how compactly written poetry can be. Read the rest of the poem, and in a second paragraph explain what you think the poet wanted us to see or to understand.

Title ____________________

Author ____________________

Prose paraphrase ____________________

Author's purpose ____________________

Name ______________________ Date ______________

2-13. A PENNY SAVED . . .

An *aphorism* is a self-evident or universally recognized truth written in a concise manner. Authors throughout history have used aphorisms to make a point, some more than others. "If at first you don't succeed, try, try again" and "A penny saved is a penny earned" are examples. Other words for *aphorism* are *maxims, axioms, morals,* and *sayings.*

Find and copy two revolutionary-era aphorisms.

1. ______________________

2. ______________________

Now write three original aphorisms that would apply to high school students today.

1. ______________________

2. ______________________

3. ______________________

Name ______________________________ Date ______________

2-14. OH, REALLY!?!

Fiction is a category of literature whose content is produced entirely or in part by the imagination and is not necessarily based on fact. Novels, short stories, and plays are in this category. Using your dictionary or textbook for any terms that you do not know, write a definition of each of the following.

TERM	DEFINITION
1. novel	______________________________
	______________________________
2. short story	______________________________
	______________________________
3. play	______________________________
	______________________________

From the literature of the Revolution found in your texts and in the chronology, list a title and author for each fiction category.

CATEGORY	TITLE AND AUTHOR
1. novel	______________________________
	______________________________
2. short story	______________________________
	______________________________
3. play	______________________________
	______________________________

Name ______________________________ Date ______________

2-15. THE TRUTH, THE WHOLE TRUTH . . .

Much of the literature of the revolutionary period was *nonfiction.* Two main types of nonfiction are the *essay* and *biography/autobiography.* In the first part of this exercise you will need to define these terms, using either your common sense, your textbook, or your dictionary.

TERM	DEFINITION
1. nonfiction	______________________________
	______________________________
2. biography	______________________________
	______________________________
3. autobiography	______________________________
	______________________________
4. essay	______________________________
	______________________________

Now see if you can name two examples of literature from this period for each category. Use your textbook or the Chronology.

CATEGORY	TITLE AND AUTHOR
1. essay	a. ______________________________
	______________________________
	b. ______________________________
	______________________________
2. biography/autobiography	a. ______________________________
	______________________________
	b. ______________________________
	______________________________

Name ______________________________ Date ______________

2-16. HEROIC COUPLET

The *heroic couplet* is a poetic device common in early American literature. A couplet is simply two lines of poetry that rhyme. The heroic couplet is one that is written in *iambic pentameter.* An *iamb* consists of two syllables, the first unaccented, the second accented (rĕ-cáll, bĕ-wáre). *Pentameter* means that there are five feet, such as an iamb, in a line of poetry. Look at this example:

N̆o róv|iṅg foót | shăll crúsh | th̆ee hére
N̆o bús|y̆ hánd | prŏvóke | ă teár.

from "The Wild Honeysuckle"
Freneau

This is a couplet, but not a heroic couplet. Why?

____

____

____

____

____

Copy a heroic couplet from the literature of this period and scan it; that is, mark its stressed and unstressed syllables and separate one iamb from another with a line.

____

____

____

____

____

Try your hand at writing your own heroic couplet. Choose a subject from nature.

____

____

____

____

____

2-17. VOCABULARY LIST

1. abdicate
2. acquiesce
3. ague
4. allure
5. amity
6. arbitrary
7. arduous
8. artifice
9. avarice
10. avert
11. celestial
12. comely
13. comport
14. despotic
15. despotism
16. disavow
17. discord
18. dissolution
19. dominion
20. endeavor
21. entreaty
22. equality
23. evince
24. exposition
25. expunge
26. forfeiture
27. formidable
28. frolicsome
29. frontier
30. frugality
31. harass
32. husbandry
33. impious
34. incorrigible
35. incur
36. inherent
37. insidious
38. insurrection
39. irresolute
40. inviolate
41. liberty
42. lineament
43. litigious
44. magnanimity
45. martial
46. mercenary
47. oppression
48. patriot
49. penury
50. perfidy
51. precept
52. precursor
53. prudent
54. rebellion
55. reconcile
56. redress
57. revere
58. revolution
59. sagacity
60. servile
61. solace
62. speculative
63. subjugate
64. sufferance
65. suffice
66. supplicate
67. temperance
68. temporal
69. transient
70. tyrant
71. unremitting
72. usurpation
73. valiant
74. venery
75. vestige

Name ______________________________ Date ______________

2-18. BEGINNINGS

An addition to a *base word,* either at the beginning or end of the word, changes its meaning. A *prefix* is added to the beginning of a word. An understanding of prefixes and their meanings can greatly increase your vocabulary. Some common prefixes are listed here.

dis—do the opposite, not
im, in, ir—not
pre—earlier, before, in advance
re—again, anew
sub—below, under, beneath
trans—across, beyond change

DIRECTIONS: Choose six words from the vocabulary list that contain prefixes. In the first set of spaces, write the root word followed by its meaning. In the second set of spaces write the word with its prefix and the new meaning. Example *moral* means honest or ethical; ***immoral*** means not honest or not ethical.

1. ______________________ means ______________________

______________________ means ______________________

2. ______________________ means ______________________

______________________ means ______________________

3. ______________________ means ______________________

______________________ means ______________________

4. ______________________ means ______________________

______________________ means ______________________

5. ______________________ means ______________________

______________________ means ______________________

6. ______________________ means ______________________

______________________ means ______________________

Name ______________________________ Date ______________

2-19. WESTWARD

Archaic Usages

An archaic word is one that has become antiquated; it is no longer current or applicable. A word still in use can also be used in an archaic way.

DIRECTIONS: Write a journal or diary entry about the frontier. You can disagree with the natives, go to Kentucky with Daniel Boone, or clear land for your new farm. Write your paragraph in the style of the day and use ten words from the vocabulary list in an archaic way. On the back of the paper define those ten words as you used them. Then substitute a more modern term or phrase for each of them.

Topic ______________________________

Entry ______________________________

Name ______________________ Date ____________

2-20. THINK IT THROUGH

Analogies

1. Frugality : Penurious ::
   A. Solace : Weeping
   B. Frontier : Seashore
   C. Country : Land
   D. Generous : Prodigal
   E. Ship : Sail
2. Comport : Deport ::
   A. Army : Martial
   B. Martial : Partial
   C. March : Walk
   D. Ashore : Country
   E. Precept : Proverb
3. Amity : Hostility ::
   A. Solace : Comfort
   B. Martial : Warlike
   C. Avarice : Generosity
   D. Country : Sky
   E. Tornado : Prairie
4. Incite : Rebellion ::
   A. Ignite: Conflagration
   B. Revolt : War
   C. Vestige : Dine
   D. Ocean : Country
   E. Frontier : Food
5. Washington : Honesty ::
   A. Sufferance : Frugality
   B. Solomon : Sagacity
   C. Peanuts : Linus
   D. George III : Benevolence
   E. Hermes : Slowness
6. Prudence : Daring ::
   A. Angry : Calm
   B. Black : Gray
   C. Joy : Glee
   D. Ill : Sick
   E. Sky : Stars

Synonyms and Antonyms

You will find a synonym and antonym answer for each word below. Mark the synonyms with an S and the antonyms with an A.

1. Servile
   A. Temperate B. Arrogant C. Submissive D. Honest E. Frugal
2. Frolicsome
   A. Somber B. Martial C. Playful D. Eager E. Easy
3. Expunge
   A. March B. Extradite C. Baffle D. Add E. Obliterate
4. Subjugate
   A. Purchase B. Subdue C. Free D. Expunge E. Assume
5. Reconcile
   A. Resolve B. Speculate C. Entreat D. Dissolve E. Embitter

Section 3
A NEW LITERATURE

1800 - 1840 Irving to Poe

SKILLS INDEX

Literary Skills		Worksheet
Atmosphere/mood	3-15	Not "A Day in June"
Biography	3-7	Dearly Departed
Characterization	3-3	The Frontiersman
	3-4	Distinctively American
	3-14	Such a Character!
	3-16	Him Again?!
Classicism	3-9	The Romantic Revolution
Humor	3-6	American Humor
Irony	3-17	How Ironic!
	3-18	Still Ironic!
Plot	3-13	The Short Story Grows Up
	3-4	Distinctively American
Romanticism	3-9	The Romantic Revolution
Setting	3-4	Distinctively American
Short story	3-13	The Short Story Grows Up
Theme	3-3	The Frontiersman

Writing Skills		Worksheet
Comparison and contrast	3-6	American Humor
	3-8	Human Rights
	3-9	The Romantic Revolution
Description	3-12	Nature—Inside and Out
	3-5	Indian Country
	3-16	Him Again?!
Exposition	3-10	One Romantic Author
Journal entry	3-12	Nature—Inside and Out
	3-5	Indian Country
Newspaper writing	3-7	Dearly Departed

Thinking Skills		Worksheet
Classifying	3-1	Growth and Change
Deductive reasoning	3-3	The Frontiersman
	3-2	Plan a Trip

	3-10	One Romantic Author
	3-13	The Short Story Grows Up
Drawing conclusions	3-15	Not "A Day in June"
Generalizing	3-4	Distinctively American
Inductive reasoning	3-9	The Romantic Revolution
Problem solving	3-2	Plan a Trip
Synthesizing	3-8	Human Rights
	3-6	American Humor

Vocabulary Skills		**Worksheet**
Analogies, synonyms, antonyms	3-20	Think It Through
Words in context	3-21	Fill In the Blank

Other Skills		**Worksheet**
Chronology	3-1	Growth and Change

WORKSHEET NOTES

3-1. Growth and Change

Literature does not exist in isolation, and an understanding of the place in history of a work of literature and its author is necessary to a mature student. This worksheet is designed to give students an overview of the history of this era as well as to encourage them to use the Chronology.

3-2. Plan a Trip

This exercise forces students to use various skills. It may prove difficult for some but could be fun. The exercise can be expanded into a longer paper, either narrative or expository in nature. Students must use historical knowledge, problem-solving, and map-reading skills. First, of course, they must choose a route. Will they go overland or choose the more common sea route through the Straits of Magellan and up the South American coast? Use of the imagination becomes imperative at this point.

3-3. The Frontiersman

Throughout our history we have had with us the people of the frontier. It seems we are always part of the "New Frontier" of a John F. Kennedy or the frontier of outer space now being explored. Mars and the moon are on the current list for possible manned exploration and colonization. Even the terms are the same. The "hero" frontiersman was often a solitary man who followed natural moral laws, for only nature and God were around to guide him. He was self-reliant, courageous, strong, good, and "rugged." He was getting a new start as he lived a life of action and danger. He was also the leader for all the people who were to come after him. Students will see this idealized figure in literature as they review the ideas of theme and characterization.

3-4. Distinctively American

While reviewing character, setting, and plot, this exercise asks students to understand why literature of the time was "A new literature" that reflected the concerns, problems, challenges, and joys of the new country.

3-5. Indian Country

This is a role-playing exercise to help students see a happening through the eyes of another person. Translating this into writing can be a valuable lesson in trying to put onto paper what is in one's head.

3-6. American Humor

Once again, students are asked to use synthesis, and comparison and contrast to see that, though there are changes, even our humor has a basis in the past.

3-7. Dearly Departed

Throughout this book, students will be asked to be aware of the different types of articles and writing styles found in a newspaper. The combination of old information and current ways of handling it, though not difficult, should help students realize that our history is, indeed, relevant and with us today. It also gives students the opportunity to learn a lot about one person from the era.

3-8. Human Rights

We are facing the same basic human rights problems today that our forebears faced; the difference is only one of degree. Students will realize that all through our history runs a thread of caring and concern for those not being treated fairly or with dignity and that human rights problems will be a continuing struggle.

3-9. The Romantic Revolution

This is a fairly easy exercise designed to help students understand a complex idea. The discussion of the exercise may involve the following ideas.

Classical literature is dominated by reason, and by the notion that using reason we can understand both man and nature, for both operate according to unchanging laws. In society, whatever is for the common good comes before personal freedom. So, classical literature reflects this order and balance; form becomes important.

Romantic literature emphasizes imagination and intuition. The spiritual truth within each individual is important and real. Countries and the people who are part of them have unlimited potential for growth and progress. Nature is beautiful, unpredictable, mysterious. It reflects the moral truths found within individuals. Romantic literature is free-flowing and ever-changing. There is room for mystery, myth, legend, superstition, and folklore. Of course, students may find some elements of both types of literature in a work written during the transition from the classical to the romantic style.

It might be interesting for students to write a composition or have a class discussion showing how the romantic philosophy met the needs of the new nation.

Exercise answers:

Classicism—unchanging laws, nature a machine, social good, clarity, common sense, resistance to change, balance, set structure

Romanticism—intuition, imagination, personal growth, individual freedom, inner perception, nature mysterious, superstition

3-10. One Romantic Author

This exercise focuses the information from the previous worksheet and offers students a chance to review and hone their expository writing skills.

3-11. National Pride

So often we emphasize the causes of the Civil War. But more than force of arms held the country together. This exercise asks students to look at the literature of the period and reflect on this aspect. Perhaps they will see a thread of national pride that extends to the present. The synthesizing required to do the work is also an important skill.

3-12. Nature – Inside and Out

This worksheet asks students to observe, describe, and synthesize, and helps prepare them for the more intense philosophies to come. The outcome will have the aspects of a journal entry.

3-13. The Short Story Grows Up

3-14. Such a Character!

3-15. Not "A Day in June"

3-16. Him Again?!

These four worksheets advance the understanding of the short story as a literary form. They continue the study begun in Section 2 and will be looked at again in future sections. The plot pattern could be a little difficult at first, but if the worksheet is used several times, the concept should become clear.

3-17. How Ironic!

3-18. Still Ironic!

Another common device is covered in these two exercises. Since the concept can be confusing for some, we will return to it in a later section.

3-19. Vocabulary List

3-20. Endings

3-21. Fill In the Blank

3-22. Think It Through

This part includes the vocabulary list and exercises dealing with words in context, suffixes, analogies, synonyms, and antonyms.

Answers

Fill In the Blank (At first glance, some of the answers seem interchangeable, but the following are most exact.)

1. authentic, decorum, impunity
2. ominous, pensive, dirge
3. surly, termagant, upbraid, temerity

Think It Through

Analogies	Synonyms	Antonyms
1. C (one who brings)	1. B	D
2. D (synonyms—specific to general)	2. E	A
3. A (common descriptions of each)	3. A	C
4. E (antonyms)	4. C	B
5. B (action and object of)	5. B	D
6. C (part of the whole)		

PROJECT IDEAS

Nobel Prize for Literature

Although the Nobel Prize was not in existence during this time period, there were many worthy candidates. Have two or three students locate the information concerning the qualifications for this prize, then award it to an American author. In an award ceremony have the students explain the reason for awarding it to that particular person. In other words, who goes to Sweden?

Class Calendar

Have several students make a large wall calendar. The entire class can work together or separately and fill it with significant anniversaries of the times, for example, the birthday of Washington Irving or the first battle of the War of 1812. This activity can be continued for future chapters.

Biography

Two or three students choose one of the first ladies of the era and report on her place in the scheme of things. Did she politic for her husband? What was her background? How did she spend her time as first lady?

Buildings

Have several students make an architectural display for the classroom. They will find pictures of notable buildings in use at this time in magazines and books. Then the students take pictures of buildings in their area that could have been built in this era or that were modeled on buildings of this era.

Research

Research the following for written or oral reports: the Capitol, War of 1812, Burr conspiracy, American flag, American privateers, U.S. naval power, black spirituals, Tripolitan War, Daniel Webster, burning of Washington, popular entertainment, Erie Canal, Underground Railroad, Seminole War, the Spanish in Florida, or any item from the Chronology.

Put on a Play

Students love to ham it up. Give them their chance. Have them dramatize a work of literature from the era. They can write a script, choose parts, design costumes and props, and perform their "original" drama for another class. Be sure to get it on videotape for posterity!

CHRONOLOGY

1790–c. 1850—The Industrial Revolution in the United States

1801—John Marshall becomes new Chief Justice of the Supreme Court

—Electoral tie, House of Representatives choose Jefferson over Burr

1801–1805—Tripolitan War in Mediterranean Sea

1802—U.S. Military Academy established at West Point

1803—Louisiana Purchase—828,000 acres added to the United States

1804–1806—Lewis and Clark expedition

1804—Nathaniel Hawthorne born

—Burr-Hamilton duel

1805–1806—Pike's expedition, sources of the Mississippi River, Colorado, and New Mexico explored

1806—Noah Webster, *Compendious Dictionary of the English Language*

1807—John Greenleaf Whittier and Henry Wadsworth Longfellow born

—Aaron Burr treason and trial

—*Clermont,* Fulton's steamship, is demonstrated on the Hudson

1808—Congress declares slave importation illegal

—Madison elected president

—Bryant, *The Embargo*

1809—Irving, *Knickerbocker's History of New York*

—Edgar Allan Poe, Oliver Wendell Holmes, and Abraham Lincoln born

1810—Annexation of West Florida

1812–1814—War of 1812

1812—Detroit and Dearborn fall

—American Academy of Natural Science founded

1813–1814—Creek Indian War

1814—Washington, D.C., captured and burned

—Battle of New Orleans

—Ghent Peace Treaty

1815—Freneau, *Poems on American Affairs*

—*North American Review* established

1816—Monroe elected president

1817—Bryant, "Thanatopsis"

1818—First Seminole War, East Florida brought under U.S. military control

1819—James Russell Lowell, Herman Melville, and Walt Whitman born

1820—Missouri Compromise

—Death penalty for U.S. citizens trading slaves

—Monroe reelected

1821—*Saturday Evening Post* founded

—Bryant, *Poems*

—Cooper, *The Spy*

1823—Cooper, *Pioneers*

—Monroe Doctrine

1824—John Quincy Adams elected president

1825—Erie Canal opens

1826—Cooper, *The Last of the Mohicans*

—Thomas Jefferson and John Adams die

1827—*Freedom's Journal*, first black newspaper

1828—Webster, *An American Dictionary of the English Language*

—Jackson elected president

—Construction of Baltimore and Ohio Railroad begins

1830—Holmes, "Old Ironsides"

—Emily Dickinson born

1831—American Anti-Slavery Society founded

—Poe, *Poems*

1832—Black Hawk War

—Jackson reelected

—Irving, *The Alhambra*

1834—Whig Party formed

1835-1842—Second Seminole War, Florida

1835—Kemble, *Journal*

—Mark Twain born; Halley's Comet sighted

1836—Bureau of Indian Affairs established

—Battles of the Alamo and San Jacinto

—Texas becomes an independent republic

—Van Buren elected president

—Morse invents the telegraph

—Bret Harte born

1837—Hawthorne, *Twice Told Tales*

1838—England and United States connected by steamship

1840—Harrison elected president

—Cooper, *The Pathfinder*

—Brook Farm founded

BIBLIOGRAPHY

Further Reading for Students and Teachers

Billington, Ray. *The Far Western Frontier: 1830-1860.* New York: Harper and Row, 1962.

Child, Lydia. *Hobomok and Other Writings on Indians.* New Brunswick, NJ: Rutgers University Press, 1824.

Cooper, James Fenimore. *Leatherstocking Saga.* New York: Avon, 1980.

Douglass, Frederick. *Narrative of the Life of Frederick Douglass, an American Slave.* New York: Penguin, 1845.

Fisher, Miles. *Negro Slave Songs in the United States.* New York: Citadel Press, 1953.

Guthrie, A. B., Jr. *The Big Sky.* New York: Bantam, 1972.

Hurwood, Bernhardt J. *My Savage Muse: The Story of My Life: Edgar Allan Poe.* Everest House, 1980.

Kelton, Elmer. *The Wolf and the Buffalo.* Boston: G. K. Hall, 1989.

Levin, Phyllis Lee. *Abigail Adams: A Biography.* New York: Ballantine, 1988.

Lifton, David S. *The Raven: A Biography of Sam Houston.* Austin: University of Texas Press, 1988.

Marrin, Albert. *Eighteen Twelve: The War Nobody Won.* New York: Macmillan, 1985.

Poe, Edgar Allan. *Tales of Terror: Ten Short Stories.* Englewood Cliffs, NJ: Prentice Hall, 1985.

Schlesinger, Arthur M., Jr. *The Age of Jackson.* Boston: Little, Brown, 1988.

Smith, Zachary. *The Battle of New Orleans.* Bowie, MD: Heritage Books, 1985.

Sugden, John. *Tecumseh's Last Stand.* Norman: University of Oklahoma Press, 1985.

Vanderwerth, W. C., ed. *Indian Oratory: A Collection of Famous Speeches by Noted Indian Chieftains.* Norman: University of Oklahoma Press, 1979.

Vidal, Gore. *Burr.* New York: Ballantine, 1988.

Name ______________________________ Date ______________

3-1. GROWTH AND CHANGE

The United States was growing and changing very quickly in its early years as an independent nation. Using the Chronology for this era and material from your texts, list changes in the following areas.

GOVERNMENT

1. ______________________
2. ______________________
3. ______________________
4. ______________________

INDUSTRY/COMMUNICATION

1. ______________________
2. ______________________
3. ______________________
4. ______________________

NATIVE AMERICANS

1. ______________________
2. ______________________
3. ______________________
4. ______________________

TRANSPORTATION

1. ______________________
2. ______________________
3. ______________________
4. ______________________

GEOGRAPHY

1. ______________________
2. ______________________
3. ______________________
4. ______________________

ARMED FORCES

1. ______________________
2. ______________________
3. ______________________
4. ______________________

Name ______________________________ Date ______________

3-2. PLAN A TRIP

You live in Boston and have heard wonderful reports about the opportunities and lifestyle in California. It is 1825. Begin planning your trip by filling in the following information.

Number of miles ______________________________

Time needed to go one way ______________________________

Types of transportation available ______________________________

____

Approximate cost ______________________________

Possible dangers along the way ______________________________

____

____

____

____

Number of suitcases and trunks allowed ______________________________

____

What to pack ______________________________

____

____

____

____

____

____

____

____

____

____

Name ______________________ Date ____________

3-3. THE FRONTIERSMAN

The United States, being a very young country at this time, was in many ways symbolized by the person out on the edge of civilization. The major themes of the literature are found in the character of the frontiersman: the importance of freedom, nature's beauty and influence, the common man, heroes in action, and the character of the frontier itself.

DIRECTIONS: Choose a character from the literature of the era and show how these five themes can be found in that person. When you have answered the following questions, you will have the basics of the "American hero."

1. Name one way in which this character demonstrated the importance of freedom. ______________________________

2. What part did nature play in this character's life? ______________________________

3. Could this character be called a "common man"? Explain. ______________________________

4. Did the character have any action in his life? Give two examples. ______________________________

5. What part did the frontier itself play in shaping his or her character? ______________________________

6. Can you name a hero in literature or real life from the twentieth century that might fit this description? ______________________________

Name ____________________ Date __________

3-4. DISTINCTIVELY AMERICAN

During this time American literature began to grow away from its European roots and form a body of writing that was unique. The distinct experiences, ideals, and beliefs of the United States made it inevitable that this would happen.

DIRECTIONS: Choose two works of literature from this era and show how they are distinctively American in the areas of setting, character, and plot. In other words, these selections were obviously written by Americans, for Americans, about Americans.

1. Title and author ____________________

   Setting (when and where) ____________________

   Main character (name and two facts about him or her) ____________________

   ____

   ____

   ____

   Plot situations (two things that happened) ____________________

   ____

   ____

   ____

2. Title and author ____________________

   Setting ____________________

   Main character ____________________

   ____

   ____

   ____

   Plot situations ____________________

   ____

   ____

   ____

Name ______________________________ Date ______________

3-5. INDIAN COUNTRY

As you can tell from the chronology, native Americans figured prominently in the events of this era as the frontier spread west, north, and south. They did appear in some of the literature of the time, but little comes to us from the native Americans themselves. Their rich and varied culture was simply not understood by the newcomers.

DIRECTIONS: You are an unusual person, a native American woman who keeps a journal. On this spring day of 1835 you spent part of the time watching a family of "whites" settle on land near your village. Write in your journal how they look, what they are doing, and how you feel about it. Continue the exercise on the back of the paper.

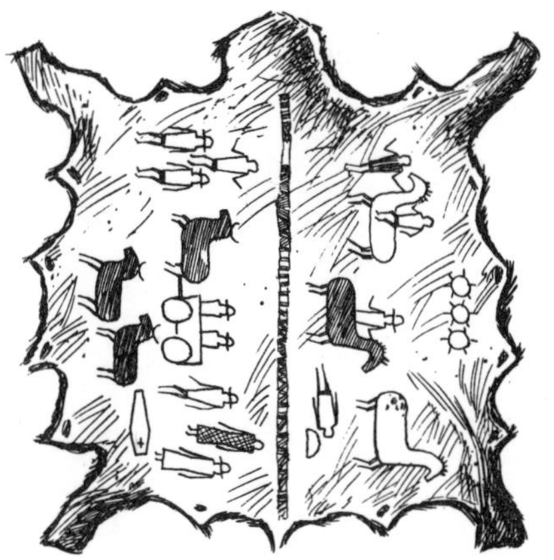

Name ______________________________ Date ______________

3-6. AMERICAN HUMOR

During this period the United States continued to develop its own sense of humor. This humor became fairly prominent in the literature of the early 1800s. We can tell much about people by what they find funny.

DIRECTIONS: Find humorous phrases, sentences, and situations in the literature of the time.

EXAMPLES	TITLE/ AUTHOR
1. ______________________	______________________
______________________	______________________
2. ______________________	______________________
______________________	______________________
3. ______________________	______________________
______________________	______________________

In what *type* of literature did you find these examples?

DIRECTIONS: Now find two examples of humor in a current written or visual source.

1. ____

____

2. ____

____

How are these two examples like or unlike the humor of the early 1800s?

Name ______________________________ Date ______________

3-7. DEARLY DEPARTED

Choose an author from this period of literature and write his or her obituary. Use an example of this type of writing from a contemporary newspaper and follow its style of writing. Notice details, sentence length, sentence structure, and word choice.

Name ____________________ Date ____________

3-8. HUMAN RIGHTS

Human rights have been a concern of Americans since Plymouth and Jamestown. The spirit of reform has been an integral part of our history. Then, as now, authors appealed to people's reason and emotions to advance a just cause.

DIRECTIONS: In the circle below, place a human rights issue of the early 1800s. In each square place a quotation regarding that subject; include the author's name.

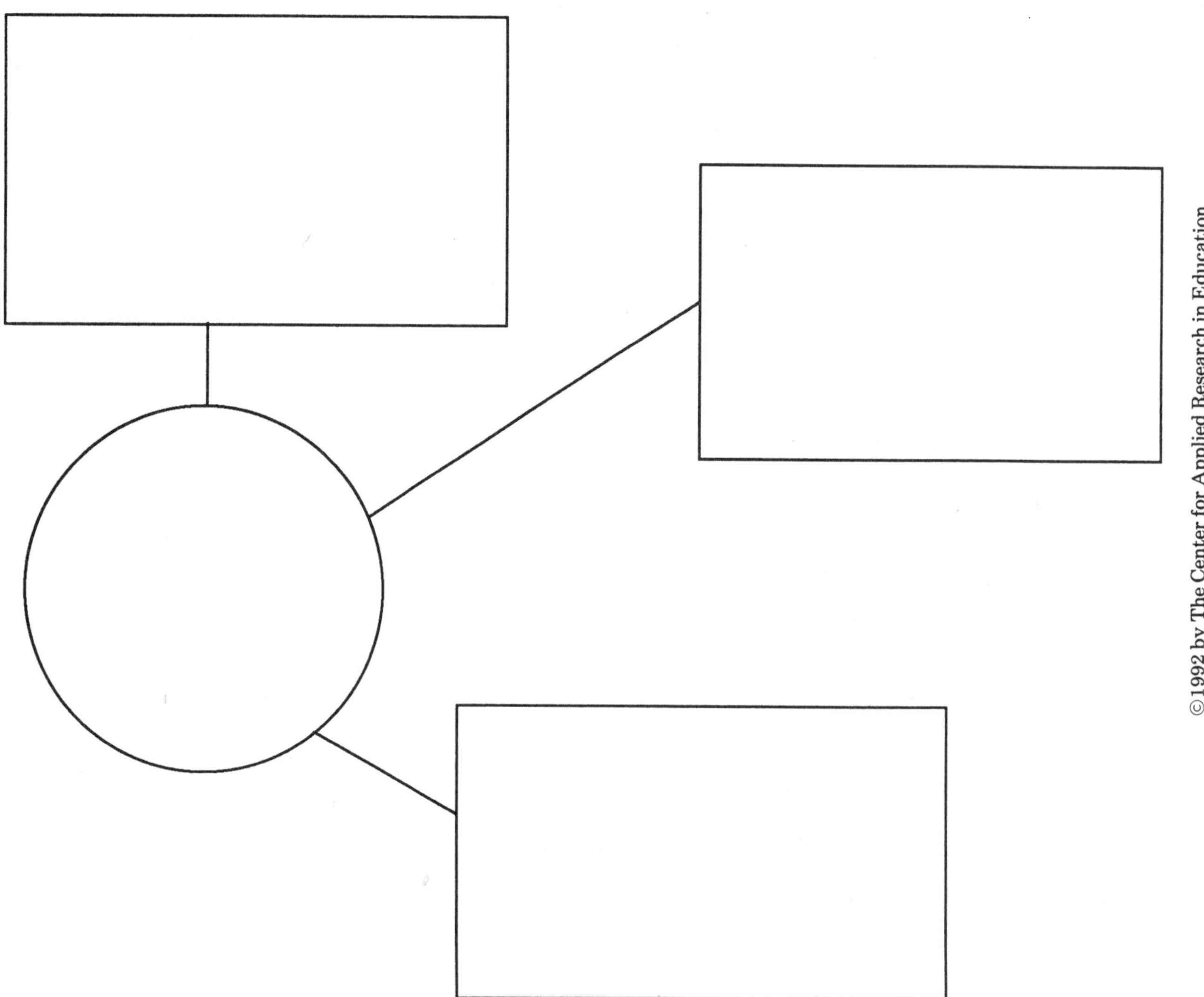

Is this issue relevant today? Explain your answer.

Name ______________________________ Date ________________

3-9. THE ROMANTIC REVOLUTION

On its way to literary independence, American culture shifted from classicism to romanticism. This was no small intellectual revolution. Below are two columns and a list of words and phrases that pertain to either classical or romantic literature. Using the words and phrases given, and your common sense and previous knowledge, place each item in the proper column.

CLASSICAL LITERATURE	ROMANTIC LITERATURE
1. reason	1. emotion
2. order	2. process, change
3.	3.
4.	4.
5.	5.
6.	6.
7.	7.
8.	8.
9.	9.
10.	10.

List: unchanging laws, intuition, nature a machine, imagination, social good, personal growth, clarity, order, spiritual growth, common sense, resistance to change, individual freedom, inner perception, nature mysterious, process, reason, emotion, superstition, balance, change, set structure

Now try your own definition of classical and romantic literature.

Name ______________________ Date ______________

3-10. ONE ROMANTIC AUTHOR

DIRECTIONS: Choose an author and list three romantic elements in his or her work. Illustrate each element with examples or quotations from the work. Concentrate also on the main character's relationship with nature. On another sheet of paper, develop these ideas into a five-paragraph composition. Choose transitions that will allow each paragraph to flow naturally into the next.

Thesis statement ______________________

____

____

Notes and examples for paragraph 1 ______________________

____

____

____

Notes and examples for paragraph 2 ______________________

____

____

____

Notes and examples for paragraph 3 ______________________

____

____

____

Conclusion (repeat and sum up the now-proven thesis statement) ______________________

____

____

____

____

____

Name ______________________________ Date ______________

3-11. NATIONAL PRIDE

Expansion, great distances, turmoil over social and governmental issues, and cultural differences all combined to convince people in Europe and America that the United States was destined to break apart. Two, or even three, countries would develop separately. However, such strong national pride existed that, for many, preserving the Union became a sacred trust. This idea was present in the literature of the era.

DIRECTIONS: Quote three passages from three different selections that show this national pride.

Title and author ______________________________

Quotation ______________________________

____

____

____

Title and author ______________________________

Quotation ______________________________

____

____

____

Title and author ______________________________

Quotation ______________________________

____

____

____

Name ______________________________ Date ______________

3-12. NATURE—INSIDE AND OUT

Many writers of this period, especially poets like Bryant, would observe and appreciate nature. Then they would work inward to become aware of the feelings evoked by the setting. Try this. Observe and record the scene outside a window or on the way to school. Note sights, sounds, weather, colors, animals, people. As you do this, note any emotions within you and record these also.

The scene ______________________________

My feelings and thoughts ______________________________

Name ______________________ Date ______________

3-13. THE SHORT STORY GROWS UP

Plot Pattern

The short story reached its full development during this period and became a distinctive American literary form. One of the main elements of the short story is *plot,* the sequence of events in the story (what happens). The basic *plot pattern* follows:

Exposition—we are introduced to the characters, places, and events from which the story arises.

Narrative hook—the plot begins; suspense is present.

Rising action—suspense increases; the main character's problems become more complicated.

Climax—suspense is greatest; emotions are high. This is the situation that, once resolved, tells us how the story will end.

Falling action—we know the outcome of the event that is the climax.

Resolution or denouement—the story ends; we know the outcome.

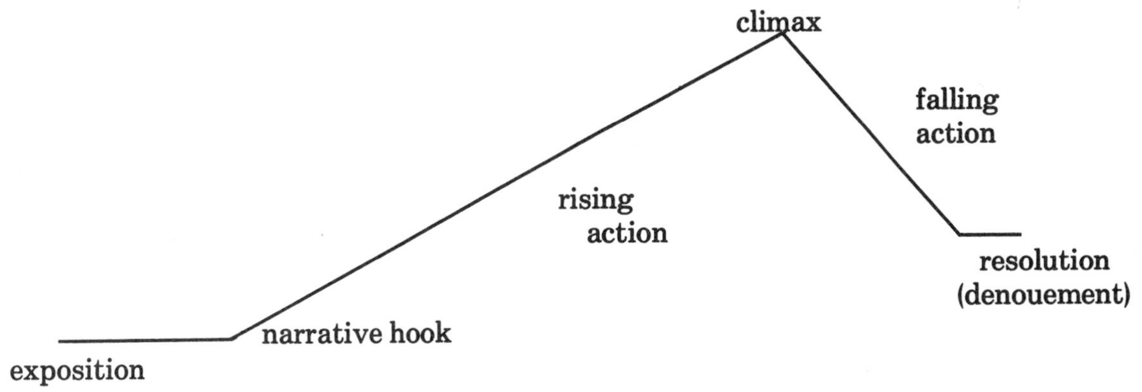

DIRECTIONS: Choose a short story from this literary period. Below and on the back of this page, name each part of the plot of your story.

____

____

____

____

____

____

____

Name ______________________________ Date ______________

3-14. SUCH A CHARACTER!

You are a great author who wants to write the biography of a famous person. Many things contribute to one's character. Begin your research by choosing a main character from one of the works you have read and filling in the chart below. You may use a fictional or nonfictional person.

NAME OF SUBJECT

Background (home life, etc.) ______________

____

____

____

____

Education ______________

____

____

____

____

Appearance ______________

____

____

____

____

Place in society ______________

____

____

____

____

Important people in life ______________

____

____

____

____

Daily activities ______________

____

____

____

____

Accomplishments ______________

____

____

____

____

Personality traits ______________

____

____

____

____

Name ______________________________ Date ______________

3-15. NOT "A DAY IN JUNE"

Atmosphere is the *mood* or emotional quality present in a work of literature. This prevailing mood is noticeable from the beginning of the story and helps establish the reader's expectations of the kind of story being read and the type of events to come. Atmosphere is often determined by setting. Word choice becomes extremely important.

DIRECTIONS: Below is the first sentence from "The Fall of the House of Usher," by Poe, with many descriptive words omitted. Fill in the blanks with words that are light and happy and that make the reader feel joy and anticipate wonderful things.

During the whole of a ______________, ______________, and ______________ day in the ______________ of the year, when the clouds ______________ in the heavens, I had been passing ______________ on horseback through a singularly ______________ tract of country, and at length found myself, as the ______________ of evening ______________ on, within view of the ______________ House of Usher.

DIRECTIONS: Now change your words to create the opposite effect. Write your answers below. Note how your mood changes. What kind of story is now expected?

1. ______________
2. ______________
3. ______________
4. ______________
5. ______________
6. ______________
7. ______________
8. ______________
9. ______________
10. ______________

Name ______________________________ Date ______________

3-16. HIM AGAIN?!

Stock characters are stereotypes, character types that occur repeatedly in written and visual stories and are quickly recognized. An example would be the "typical" Englishman with an extremely educated accent and a monocle who is quite stuffy and not a little pompous. Then, of course, there is the cowboy who says little but means every word. (His gun tends to speak quite eloquently, however.)

DIRECTIONS: Name three stock characters from television and write three adjectives describing them.

1. Name ______________________________

   Adjectives ____________, ____________, ____________

2. Name ______________________________

   Adjectives ____________, ____________, ____________

3. Name ______________________________

   Adjectives ____________, ____________, ____________

DIRECTIONS: Now choose three stock characters from the literature of this era and write three adjectives for each. (Hint: Check works of Washington Irving.)

1. Name ______________________________

   Adjectives ____________, ____________, ____________

2. Name ______________________________

   Adjectives ____________, ____________, ____________

3. Name ______________________________

   Adjectives ____________, ____________, ____________

DIRECTIONS: Choose one of the characters mentioned above and write a one-paragraph composition describing them. Use your three adjectives as the basis of the description. Complete your writing on the back of this page.

Name ______________________________ Date ______________

3-17. HOW IRONIC!

One type of irony is *verbal* or *rhetorical* irony, saying the opposite of what is meant.

Examples: The day is cold, wet and dreary. You say to a friend, "Isn't this a beautiful day!"
An acquaintance does something underhanded and nasty. You say, "Well, that was nice! You're a real prince!"
As you can see, *sarcasm* is a type of irony.

DIRECTIONS: Find two examples of verbal irony in the literature of this period. Explain what makes them ironic.

Example 1 ______________________________

____

____

Explanation ______________________________

____

____

____

Example 2 ______________________________

____

____

Explanation ______________________________

____

____

____

DIRECTIONS: Write two original examples of verbal or rhetorical irony.

1. ______________________________

____

2. ______________________________

____

Name ______________________________ Date ______________

3-18. STILL IRONIC!

Dramatic, tragic, or *situational irony* occurs when the reader or viewer knows more about an incident than does a character involved in it. Thus, a statement or incident can have a different or additional meaning for the reader. The author relies on the reader's intelligence to spot the real meaning.

Examples: You say to a friend, "I have decided to join the gang for the field trip after all." Your friend knows that the bus just left.
A friend says, "I have decided to mend my quarrel with Joseph so that we can be friends again."
You have just learned that Joseph has been killed in an accident.

DIRECTIONS: Find two examples of situational irony in the literature of this period. Explain what makes the example ironic.

Example 1 ______________________________

Explanation ______________________________

Example 2 ______________________________

Explanation ______________________________

DIRECTIONS: Write one example of situational, dramatic, or tragic irony.

3-19. VOCABULARY LIST

1. abscond
2. accost
3. approbation
4. ascertain
5. audacity
6. auspicious
7. authentic
8. beguiling
9. bestow
10. blight
11. boon
12. carrion
13. chastise
14. classical
15. conciliatory
16. craven
17. cupola
18. decorum
19. definitive
20. desolation
21. detrimental
22. dirge
23. discordant
24. draught
25. ebony
26. epoch
27. expedient
28. fabrication
29. forlorn
30. hoary
31. immolate
32. impediment
33. impregnable
34. impunity
35. inexorably
36. inflexible
37. inimitable
38. innate
39. melancholy
40. mien
41. obdurate
42. obliterate
43. ocular
44. ominous
45. pall
46. panoply
47. parsimony
48. pensive
49. placid
50. pliant
51. precarious
52. prevalent
53. prodigious
54. pursue
55. quaff
56. querulous
57. rancor
58. redress
59. retribution
60. shroud
61. sobriquet
62. solicitude
63. speculate
64. superfluous
65. surly
66. tacit
67. tantalized
68. temerity
69. termagant
70. trepidation
71. upbraid
72. venerable
73. virtuoso
74. visage
75. vulnerable

Name ______________________________ Date ______________

3-20. ENDINGS

A *suffix* is added to the end of a *base word* or *root* to form a new word. An understanding of suffixes and their meanings can greatly increase your vocabulary. Some common suffixes are listed here.

able—able to, capable, worthy of (respectable)

ant, ent—one who, being in a specified state or condition (confident)

ate, ite—associated with, characterized by (suburbanite)

ion, tion, ation—act of, state of being, action or process (expectation, tension)

ive—performing or having a tendency to a specified action (demonstrative)

ly—like, in the nature of (sisterly)

ous—like, full of, possessing (joyous)

DIRECTIONS: Choose six words from the vocabulary list that have suffixes. In the first set of spaces, write the root word followed by its meaning. In the second set of spaces, write the word with its suffix and the new meaning.

1. ______________________ means ______________________

   ______________________ means ______________________

2. ______________________ means ______________________

   ______________________ means ______________________

3. ______________________ means ______________________

   ______________________ means ______________________

4. ______________________ means ______________________

   ______________________ means ______________________

5. ______________________ means ______________________

   ______________________ means ______________________

6. ______________________ means ______________________

   ______________________ means ______________________

Name ______________________________ Date ______________

3-21. FILL IN THE BLANK

DIRECTIONS: Twelve of the vocabulary words are listed below. Fill in the blanks in each sentence from the list. Each word is used once.

Answer List:
temerity, authentic, ominous, pensive, termagant, decorum, dirge, upbraid, impunity, surly

1. When Jack spotted the ______________ 1957 T-Bird, he lost all sense of ______________ as he trampled people with ______________ in his eagerness to reach the car.
2. As ______________ clouds built up on the western horizon, the ______________ funeral procession walked to the sound of a melancholy ______________ toward the church seen ahead in the distant valley.
3. The ______________ ______________ would constantly ______________ her husband with ______________, even in front of strangers.

DIRECTIONS: Now write two sentences of your own. In each use at least three of the vocabulary words. Underline each word that you use from the vocabulary list.

1. ____

____

____

____

____

2. ____

____

____

____

____

____

Name ______________________________ Date ______________

3-22 THINK IT THROUGH

Analogies

1. Retribution : Nemesis ::
   A. Venerable : Cathedral
   B. Ominous : Spring
   C. Aid : Benefactor
   D. Ocular : Eyes
   E. Rancor : Joy
2. Parsimony : Stinginess ::
   A. Country : Sky
   B. Nose : Ocular
   C. Termagant : Shrew
   D. Virtuoso : Talented
   E. Vulnerable : Guarded
3. Greece : Classical ::
   A. America : Democratic
   B. Peru : Mountains
   C. France : Wine
   D. England : Island
   E. Mexico : Peso
4. Placid : Disturbed ::
   A. Precarious : Unsafe
   B. Pliant : Ominous
   C. Desolation : Rome
   D. Temerity : Mouse
   E. Surly : Courteous
5. Chastise : Offender ::
   A. Revolt : War
   B. Quaff : Drink
   C. Redress : Dress
   D. Spring : Run
   E. Speculate : Guess
6. Cupola : Church ::
   A. Cathedral : Large
   B. Termagant : Shrew
   C. Battle : War
   D. Spring : Autumn
   E. Rancor : Anger

Synonyms and Antonyms

You will find a synonym and antonym answer for each word below. Mark the synonyms with an S and the antonyms with an A.

1. Craven
   A. Surly B. Cowardly C. Stubborn D. Courageous E. Frugal

2. Definitive
   A. Indecisive B. Tumult C. Corrupt D. Approbation E. Conclusive

3. Superfluous
   A. Unnecessary B. Powerful C. Required D. Fluent E. Lost

4. Impediment
   A. Umbrella B. Encouragement C. Hindrance D. Column E. Prevalent

5. Termagant
   A. Orange B. Shrew C. Insect D. Helpmate E. Tree

Section 4

INDEPENDENCE IN LITERATURE

1840 - 1870 Emerson to Alcott

SKILLS INDEX

	4-9	Civil War
	4-8	Seekers
Problem solving	4-8	Seekers
	4-5	My Walden Pond
Synthesizing	4-1	Transcendentalism
	4-2	Puritanism—Still Here
	4-3	Trust Thyself
	4-5	My Walden Pond
	4-6	People Care

Vocabulary Skills		**Worksheet**
Abstract words	4-20	Concrete and Abstract
Analogies, synonyms, antonyms	4-21	Think It Through
Concrete words	4-20	Concrete and Abstract
Word combinations	4-17	1 + 1 = 1
	4-18	Vocabulary List
	4-19	Crossword

WORKSHEET NOTES

4-1. Transcendentalism

4-2. Puritanism—Still Here

The first of these worksheets helps students understand a new philosophy; the second reminds them of an older, founding philosophy. To a certain extent, we are a product of both. Emerson, Thoreau, Alcott, Crockett, and Sanford, among others, show many elements of the newer thinking; Hawthorne and Melville especially embody many of the pessimistic Puritan ways of looking at the human race. The correct use of quotation marks could also be taught with these exercises.

4-3. Trust Thyself

Using the skills of synthesizing, and comparison and contrast, students are asked to relate the admired American qualities of the past to people of today. They should find it easy to name three people with the frontier qualities of individualism and self-reliance and, perhaps, to understand more about our characteristics as a nation.

4-4. An Author's Philosophy

Whether the teacher chooses the author or has the students do so, this exercise not only helps students come to grips with one person's way of looking at life and handling problems but also gives them further practice writing a meaningful expository composition. If the teacher suggests that the students use this exercise to describe their own philosophy, they may be intrigued with analyzing the way they look at life. The composition could become an autobiography.

4-5. My Walden Pond

This exercise allows students to use Thoreau as a model to understand something of themselves and the practicalities of fulfilling dreams and wishes. This could be expanded into a diary modeled on Thoreau's.

4-6. People Care

The most obvious descendants of this era, especially of Thoreau and his theory of civil disobedience, would be Gandhi and Martin Luther King, Jr. Others will come to mind as students begin to make comparisons. This thinking should, once again, demonstrate our roots in the past.

4-7. From the Editor

This exercise, like the previous one, shows our relationships to the past and allows students to expand their knowledge of writing styles found in a newspaper. This will also aid them in becoming discriminating writers and readers. Provide students with one or more sample editorials from which to study format and style.

4-8. Seekers

Students are asked to focus not only on the changes in society but also on how these changes affected people. By using two hundred fictitious people, perhaps students will understand that real people were involved, not some amorphous mass with no personality, no problems, no passions. If the students cannot think of ten jobs or cannot find them in the literature of the era, the Chronology contains some clues.

4-9. Civil War

Students should note the lack of the hatred and anger directed at the other side in the literature for this exercise. Along with being used to guide students through an expository composition, this worksheet could be used to review such characteristics of a formal paper as correct punctuation (especially quotation marks) spelling, and how the paper itself should be presented (i.e., unlined paper, typed or in ink, correct margins, one side of the paper only, placement of the title, etc.).

4-10. Manifest Destiny

If a student is to paraphrase the ideas of another person accurately, that student must not only understand thoroughly what the author is saying but also be able to read between the lines to grasp emotions involved. In this case, an understanding of the historical context will help.

4-11. Larger Than Life

Imagination plays a huge role in tall tales, and here students get to put theirs to use by making up their own tall-tale character. The only limitation is that they depict the characteristics of individualism and self-reliance.

4-12. I Say So!

4-13. He Says So!

4-14. I Know Everything

These three exercises work together to give students additional understanding in the use of point of view. Point of view is carefully considered by an author, and students need to know this. In regard to the last section in Worksheet 4-14, teachers could ask why that point of view was the best one for a particular story. By the time they reach that part of the exercises, students should be able to give a thoughtful answer.

4-15. What Next?

Students should know that in good literature there is no such thing as a surprise ending; often the clues are just hidden a bit more. During this study of foreshadowing, teachers could point out that there are different degrees of suspense, ranging from mild curiosity to screaming horror.

4-16. Formal or Informal

This is a very basic exercise designed to help students understand a very diversified literary form. But even this basis requires them to look at writing style and word choice and the necessity for consistency. Students might be asked if their own essays have demonstrated consistency in these areas. Chances are, many students haven't even thought of their own writing style in these areas.

4-17. 1 + 1 = 1

Possible answers:

Cattle Ranching—cowboy, cowgirl, cowpuncher, bunkhouse, round up, branding iron, ranch house, windmill

All-American—baseball, first baseman, shortstop, left field, grandstand, double play foul ball, home plate

"New" Names—New York, New Haven, New Orleans, New Jersey, New Iberia, Newport, New Ulm, New Rochelle, New Holland

"ville" Names—Louisville, Catonsville, Knoxville, Brownsville, Jacksonville, Gainesville, Holdenville, Barnesville, Mayville, Centerville

4-18. Vocabulary List

4-19. Crossword

4-20. Concrete and Abstract

4-21. Think It Through

This is the vocabulary study part of the section. The crossword is a game that is for fun as well as for using thinking skills for word definitions. The solution is below. An understanding of concrete and abstract words is necessary for an accurate analysis of the philosophies and essays so prevalent during this era. Sample answers for concrete words are bastion, diadem, lattice, lintel, sachem, visage. Possible abstract answers are ludicrous, obsequious, placid, churlish, autocratic.

The answers for "Think It Through" follow. By this time, students will be seeing different types of relationships in the analogies.

Answers

Crossword

Think It Through

Analogies	Synonyms	Antonyms
1. C (opposites)	1. C	A
2. B (synonyms)	2. E	B
3. E (whole to part)	3. C	A
4. A (degree of difference)	4. D	C
5. C (action and object of)	5. B	E
6. D (leaders of)		

PROJECT IDEAS

Throw a Party

Plan a party for one of the authors of the era. Match the decorations and food to the author's lifestyle and beliefs. Draw up a guest list.

Make a Poster

Have a small group of students make a large poster championing one of the causes of the Civil War period. It would be interesting to have two or three groups choose opposing ideas for their posters.

Research

Research the following for oral or written reports: Walden Pond today, John James Audubon, John Brown's raid, the "Bloomers," a key Civil War battle, a plantation, the Seneca Falls Convention, immigration, a native American incident, the practice of medicine, the Hudson River school of painting, factory conditions, the rise of labor unions or any other item from the Chronology.

Time for a Play

Have a group of students reenact an incident from the times. The group can write its own dialogue. Filming this for posterity or to show to another class can be interesting.

It Pays to Advertise

Choose a newly invented product of the time and plan an advertising campaign to introduce it to the masses. Part of the plan would be two one-minute radio spots aimed at specific consumer groups.

Native Americans—Where Are They?

Two or three students could locate the pre-Manifest Destiny tribes on a map and either enlarge the map or draw one for classroom display.

Maxims

Collect a list of maxims from different times and places, including the era being studied, for classroom display. These could be printed neatly and posted in various places in the room. The author's name should be included. The sayings of Confucius would be a good starting point.

CHRONOLOGY

1840-1846—Father DeSmet founds missions in Oregon throughout the Plains

1841—Brook Farm experiment begun

1844—Polk elected president

—Telegraph company organized by Morse and others

1845—Texas is annexed

1846-1848—War with Mexico

1846—Melville, *Typee*

—Iowa admitted to the Union

1847—First Mormons in the valley of the Great Salt Lake

—Emerson, *Poems*

1848—California Gold Rush

—First Women's Rights Convention, Seneca Falls, New York

1849—W. Hunt invents the safety pin

1850—Hawthorne, *The Scarlet Letter*

—*Harper's Magazine* founded

—California admitted to the Union

—territories of Utah and New Mexico formed

1851—Pierce elected president

—Melville, *Moby Dick*

—Hawthorne, *The House of Seven Gables*

1852—Stowe, *Uncle Tom's Cabin*

—First passenger elevator invented by Otis; skyscrapers now possible

1853—Gadsden Purchase

—New York and Chicago connected by rail

1854—Thoreau, *Walden*

—Japan reopened by Perry

—Kansas and Nebraska territories organized

1856—Buchanan elected president

—Woodrow Wilson born

1857—Dred Scott decision

—Lincoln-Douglas debates

1858—Theodore Roosevelt born

—Minnesota admitted to the Union

—Pikes Peak Gold Rush

1859—Harper's Ferry raided by John Brown

1860—Repeating rifle introduced by Winchester

—Gold discovered in Idaho and Montana

1861-1865—Civil War

1861—Abraham Lincoln elected president

—South Carolina secedes; ten states follow

—Davis elected president of the Confederacy

—First battle of Bull Run

—Kansas admitted to the Union

—Cheyenne-Arapaho War, Chivington Massacre

1862—Revolving machine gun perfected by Gatling

—Battles of Antietam, second Bull Run, Fredericksburg

1863—Emancipation Proclamation

—The Gettysburg Address

—Alcott, *Hospital Sketches*

—West Virginia admitted to the Union

—First conscription act

—Battles of Chancellorsville, Vicksburg, Gettysburg, Chickamauga, Lookout Mountain, Missionary Ridge

1864—Thoreau, *The Maine Woods*

—Battles of the Wilderness, Spotsylvania, others

—Sherman's march to the sea

—Lincoln reelected

1865—Lee's surrender to Grant at Appomattox Courthouse

—Lincoln assassinated

—Thirteenth Amendment ratified (slavery abolished)

—Great cattle drives from Texas to railroads in Kansas and Nebraska begin

1867—Lanier, *Tiger Lilies*

—Alaska purchased

—Nebraska admitted to the Union

—Oklahoma reservation established for the Five Tribes

—Sioux reservation established in the Black Hills

1868—Johnson impeachment missed by one vote

—Grant elected president

1869—Cross-continential railroad completed, Promontory, Utah

—Nevada admitted to the Union

—Electric voting machine invented, Edison

1870—Ku Klux Klan founded

BIBLIOGRAPHY

Further Reading for Students and Teachers

Alger, Horatio, Jr. *The Young Patriots: Six Brave Boys in the Civil War.* Boynton Beach, FL: G. K. Westgard, 1987.

Catton, Bruce. *American Goes to War.* Hanover, NH: Wesleyan University Press, 1958.

Crane, Stephen. *Red Badge of Courage.* Englewood Cliffs, NJ: Prentice Hall, 1987.

Dunlay, Thomas W. *Wolves for the Blue Soldiers.* Baton Rouge: Louisiana State University Press.

Faulkner, William. *Unvanquished.* New York: Random House, 1966.

Field, Rachel. *All This and Heaven Too.* Cutchogue, NY: Buccaneer Books, 1983.

Foote, Shelby. *The Civil War: A Narrative.* New York: Random House, 1986.

Griffith, Elisabeth. *In Her Own Right: The Life of Elizabeth Cady Stanton.* New York: Oxford University Press, 1984.

Higginson, Thomas W. *Army Life in a Black Regiment.* New York: Norton, 1984.

Jaynes, G. *The Killing Ground.* Needham Heights, MA: Silver, Burdett and Ginn, 1986.

Jones, Katharine M., ed. *Heroines of Dixie: Spring of High Hope.* Saint Simons Island, GA: Mockingbird Books, 1983.

Magoffin, Susan C. *Down the Santa Fe Trail and into Mexico: The Diary of Susan Shelby Magoffin, 1846-1847.* Lincoln: University of Nebraska Press, 1982.

McLuhan, T. C. *Touch the Earth: A Self-portrait of Indian Existence.* New York: Simon and Schuster, 1971.

Mitchell, Margaret. *Gone with the Wind.* New York: Avon, 1976.

Rawls, Walton, ed. *Great Civil War Heroes and Their Battles.* New York: Abbeville Press, 1985.

Seidman, Laurence Ivan. *Once in the Saddle: The Cowboy's Frontier, 1866-1896.* New York: Mentor Books, 1977.

Taylor, Susie K. *A Black Woman's War Memoirs.* New York: Wiener, 1988.

Name ______________________________ Date ______________

4-1. TRANSCENDENTALISM

A new, optimistic philosophy gained preeminence during this era. Ralph Waldo Emerson was primarily responsible for the statement of these ideas, which found expression in much of the literature of the time.

DIRECTIONS: Listed below are five ideas from the transcendental philosophy. Quote a passage from the literature of the time to illustrate each one. Use at least two different authors.

1. The individual human being is basically good.

____

____

____

2. Humans have free will.

____

____

____

3. The spiritual reality, not the material world, is important.

____

____

____

4. Spiritual reality and guidance comes from within, and one has only to listen to this "higher self" or intuition to gain truth.

____

____

____

5. Individuality and self-reliance are important characteristics of a "whole" individual.

____

____

____

Name ______________________ Date ______________

4-2. PURITANISM—STILL HERE

Puritanism had all but disappeared as a religion, having been replaced by Unitarianism and Congregationalism. Nevertheless, the religion of the Pilgrims still remained powerful in the hearts and minds of many people. This philosophy (theology) is present in some of the best literature of the mid-1800s.

DIRECTIONS: Listed below are five ideas that have their origin in Puritanism. Quote a passage from the literature of the times to illustrate each one. Use at least two different authors.

1. Sin and guilt play a large part in our lives.

____

____

____

2. Humans are born with original sin and are, therefore, basically sinful and depraved.

____

____

____

3. A person's fate is determined by outside forces and only an outside force (God?) can save us.

____

____

____

4. Life is a struggle between good and evil, which are intertwined. (An inner struggle is often depicted.)

____

____

____

5. Evil often takes the form of social injustices, so reform should be pursued zealously.

____

____

____

Name ______________________________ Date ________________

4-3. TRUST THYSELF

The frontier qualities of individualism and self-reliance permeated American society. Using your common sense and knowledge of history and literature, describe one historical figure who is a self-reliant individualist. What qualities does he or she have? Then name three well-known people from today whom you would consider individualists. In two or three sentences tell why you chose them.

Description ______________________________

____

____

____

____

____

____

____

____

____

Person 1 ______________________________

____

____

____

Person 2 ______________________________

____

____

____

Person 3 ______________________________

____

____

____

Name ______________________________ Date ________________

4-4. AN AUTHOR'S PHILOSOPHY

Everyone at one time or another faces moral struggles. Some involve social justice: others involve looking for a way to live a life of integrity, courageously and honestly. During the mid-1800s, with so many changes in life and society, these searches and struggles were especially prominent in the literature. A reader can learn much about an author through his or her writings and, perhaps, gain some personal answers.

DIRECTIONS: Choose a work by one author and analyze his or her philosophy by filling in the information below. Then, using this information as a rough draft, on the back of this sheet write an essay describing your author's philosophy.

Title and author ______________________________

What part does nature play in life? ______________________________

____

____

To whom or what does one turn for guidance? (Prove it with a quotation.)

____

____

Who is in control of one's life? ______________________________

____

Is the view of life optimistic or pessimistic? (Prove it.) ______________________________

____

____

____

What is the main problem with which the author deals? ______________________________

____

How is the answer found? ______________________________

What is the answer to this particular problem? ______________________________

____

Name ______________________ Date ______________

4-5. MY WALDEN POND

Henry David Thoreau had his special place where he could learn, grow, write, and be self-reliant and happy. Everyone has an idea of what a personal place like this would be.

DIRECTIONS: Locate your special place and fill in the information in the spaces.

Location ______________________

Description ______________________

____

____

____

____

Activities ______________________

____

____

____

____

Visitors allowed ______________________

____

____

____

____

Activities and amount of time ______________________

____

____

____

____

Budget (to begin the adventure)

Item	Cost
1. ______________	________
2. ______________	________
3. ______________	________
4. ______________	________
5. ______________	________

Total set-up cost ______________________

Daily expenses ______________________

Name ______________________________ Date ______________

4-6. PEOPLE CARE

From the beginning, the United States had a history of commitment to social justice. The 1800s were no exception. Even with the expansion of borders, the settlement of the West, a foreign war, and a Civil War, people found time to be feminists, abolitionists, utopians, labor unionists, and many other "ists." These social movements were an expression of old and new beliefs.

DIRECTIONS: Choose three authors of the period and determine the social cause in which they were more interested. Then choose a person from the twentieth century that would be most like that author and tell one or two things about him or her.

Author ______________________________ Cause ______________

Name from twentieth century ______________________________

Description ______________________________

____

____

____

____

Author ______________________________ Cause ______________

Name from twentieth century ______________________________

Description ______________________________

____

____

____

____

Author ______________________________ Cause ______________

Name from twentieth century ______________________________

Description ______________________________

____

____

____

Name ______________________________ Date ______________

4-7. FROM THE EDITOR

As an editorial writer of the mid-1800s, it is imperative that you think through the controversial issues of the day and form your point of view. Choose an issue (women's rights, slavery, North vs. South, etc.) and form your opinions. Following the writing style of a major editorial in a daily newspaper, take a stand, write out your ideas and reasons for it, and persuade your readers that your opinion is correct. Notice the length, writing style, and arrangement of ideas in your sample editorial. Use this paper, front and back, to write your rough draft. The final copy will be neatly done on an attached sheet.

Topic ______________________________

Title of article ______________________________

Editorial ______________________________

Name ______________________________ Date ______________

4-8. SEEKERS

During this time, immigration to the United States was increasing. Irish, German, Scandinavian, British, Italian, and other European citizens came looking for a new start. The Treaty of Guadalupe Hidalgo permitted Mexican citizens to remain in annexed and acquired territories as U.S. citizens if they wished. Newcomers were also arriving in smaller numbers from places such as China, the West Indies, Canada, and South and Latin America.

DIRECTIONS: List ten jobs or careers that these newcomers could fill in an ever-expanding United States.

1. ______________________
2. ______________________
3. ______________________
4. ______________________
5. ______________________
6. ______________________
7. ______________________
8. ______________________
9. ______________________
10. ______________________

DIRECTIONS: If 200 immigrants arrived at one time, how many do you think would be needed to fill each of the jobs that you listed above? Write the number after each listing; make certain the total equals 200.

DIRECTIONS: Now decide where these 200 people would live. List six locations and allocate them properly. Again, make certain that the total adds up to 200.

	LOCATION	NUMBER
1.	______________________	________
2.	______________________	________
3.	______________________	________
4.	______________________	________
5.	______________________	________
6.	______________________	________

Name ______________________________ Date ______________

4-9. CIVIL WAR

People's writing during the tragedy of the Civil War shows the emotions they felt. Abraham Lincoln, Robert E. Lee, Louisa May Alcott, and many others left letters, speeches, poems, and journals that expressed their feelings.

DIRECTIONS: Choose the writings of two participants in the Civil War and use those writings as the basis of a composition showing the emotions evoked by the war. Your thesis statement will indicate that your subjects' feelings and inner struggles typify the general feelings regarding the war. The second and third paragraphs may detail two of these emotions and what aroused them. The fourth paragraph will generalize about the war's effect on people in general. The fifth will conclude the paper by summing up your ideas in such a way as to show that your thesis was correct. Use this paper, front and back, as scratch paper for a rough draft. Write your final draft very neatly on another sheet of paper.

Authors and titles to be used ______________________________

____

Thesis statement ______________________________

____

____

Paragraph 2 (main idea and supporting information)

Paragraph 3 (main idea and supporting information)

Paragraph 4 (main idea and supporting information)

Paragraph 5 (conclusion)

Name ____________________ Date ____________

4-10. MANIFEST DESTINY

Many felt that it was the "manifest destiny" of the United States to settle and claim the entire continent. Providence had allocated the land to them to be home to a quickly increasing population. Railroads were being established, land settled, and gold was discovered in several areas. But what about the native Americans?

DIRECTIONS: Below are quotations from two native Americans.* Using them or two from your text, paraphrase them. Try to keep the same emotions, but use your own words. Use the back of this paper or a separate sheet.

The White people never cared for land or deer or bear. When we Indians kill meat, we eat it all up. When we dig roots we make little holes. When we built houses, we make little holes. When we burn grass for grasshoppers, we don't ruin things. We shake down acorns and pinenuts. We don't chop down trees. We only use dead wood. But the White people plow up the ground, pull down the trees, kill everything. The tree says, "Don't. I am sore. Don't hurt me." But they chop it down and cut it up. The spirit of the land hates them. They blast out trees and stir it up to its depths. They saw up the trees. That hurts them. The Indians never hurt anything, but the White people destroy all. They blast rocks and scatter them on the ground. The rock says, "Don't. You are hurting me." But the White people pay no attention. When the Indians use rocks, they take little round ones for their cooking. . . . How can the spirit of the earth like the White man? . . . Everywhere the White man has touched, it is sore.

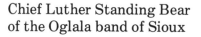

Wintu holy woman

We did not think of the great open plains, the beautiful rolling hills, and winding streams with tangled growth, as "wild." Only to the white man was nature a "wilderness" and only to him was the land "infested" with "wild" animals and "savage" people. To us it was tame. Earth was bountiful and we were surrounded with the blessings of the Great Mystery. Not until the hairy man from the east came and with brutal frenzy heaped injustices upon us and the families we loved was it "wild" for us. When the very animals of the forest began fleeing from his approach, then it was that for us the "Wild West" began.

Chief Luther Standing Bear
of the Oglala band of Sioux

*From *Touch the Earth* by T. C. McLuhan, © 1971 by Touchstone Press, a division of Simon & Schuster. Used by permission.

Name ________________________________ Date ______________

4-11. LARGER THAN LIFE

Tall tales have had a prominent place in American literature from the beginning. They are a humorous depiction of the ideals of self-reliance and individualism. These American heroes may brag, exaggerate, use substandard English (horrors!) and may, at times, be totally obnoxious; however, they are very good at what they do.

DIRECTIONS: Choose a tall-tale hero such as Paul Bunyan, Davy Crockett, Mike Fink, or Pecos Bill and describe him (i.e., appearance, personality traits, and special skills).

Name ________________________________

Description ________________________________

DIRECTIONS: Now, make up your own tall-tale hero and describe him or her as you have done above.

Name ________________________________

Description ________________________________

Name ______________________________ Date ______________

4-12. I SAY SO!

Point of view is the position from which the author of a short story or novel tells us what happened. If the story is told to us by someone within the story using such first-person pronouns as *I, we, me, my, mine, our,* the author is using the *first-person point of view.* This vantage can take the reader into the story, and the author can speak directly to him or her. However, with this point of view we know only what the character knows, and this knowledge can be incomplete or even inaccurate.

DIRECTIONS: Tell about an incident in which you were involved. You do this all the time; pretend you are telling it to a friend.

____

____

____

____

____

____

____

____

____

DIRECTIONS: Now look back over your story. What information does your reader or listener not know? List three things.

____

____

____

____

____

____

____

____

____

Name ________________________________ Date ________________

4-13. HE SAYS SO!

Another position from which the author will tell his or her story is from the *third-person point of view.* The author will step out of the story and watch it from the point of view of one of the characters within the story. Therefore, this is a limited point of view because we are restricted to what that character says, sees, and hears. The author will use such third-person pronouns as *he, she, it, they* and *them* to tell the story.

DIRECTIONS: Take the story you told from the first-person point of view and change it to third person. Step outside the story and watch it through the eyes of another person in the story. Watch your pronouns.

DIRECTIONS: Look back over your story. Now what information does your reader or listener *not* know. List three things.

Name ______________________________ Date ______________

4-14. I KNOW EVERYTHING!

An author may choose to play God and show us the story from the *omniscient point of view. Omniscient* means all-knowing, so we not only know what people say and do, but we also know what is going on in their hearts and minds. The author can comment on all of the characters, show us any event he or she wants, and stop the story to give us information if he or she chooses. The author can do anything because he or she knows everything.

DIRECTIONS: Now the challenge—you are omniscient. Tell your story again from the omniscient point of view. You could find this difficult to relate in so short a space because you know so much.

____

____

____

____

____

____

____

____

____

____

____

____

____

____

____

DIRECTIONS: Choose three selections from your text, one for each of the three points of view. Write the title, author and point of view.

1. ______________________________

2. ______________________________

3. ______________________________

Name ______________________________ Date ______________

4-15. WHAT NEXT?

Every story has an element of suspense, something that makes us wonder what will happen next. One of the ways in which suspense is created is through the use of *foreshadowing.* This occurs when an author drops hints about what is coming. If we are reading a story written by a good author and we are astute readers, there should be no real surprises in a story; everything will have been accounted for in advance. Even the setting and mood set early in a story, such as in Edgar Allan Poe's works, are part of foreshadowing.

DIRECTIONS: Choose one story from this time period. Find four hints early in the story that prepare us for what is to follow. The weather, something that concerns a character, or an unpleasant personality trait can foretell future events.

Clue 1 ______________________________

____

____

Clue 2 ______________________________

____

____

Clue 3 ______________________________

____

____

Clue 4 ______________________________

____

____

DIRECTIONS: Now show how two of these clues proved true as the story progressed.

Clue 1 ______________________________

____

____

Clue 2 ______________________________

____

____

Name ______________________________ Date ______________

4-16. FORMAL OR INFORMAL

The *essay* is a short, nonfiction composition on any subject that attempts to discuss a topic or opinion or to persuade us to a course of action. This type of writing can be divided into two main types, formal and informal. The *formal essay,* sometimes called an *article,* is serious, well organized, and impersonal, and the language used is usually dignified. An *informal essay* is more relaxed and personal. It often has a rambling structure, and the topics can be humorous and unusual. Self-revelation often occurs.

DIRECTIONS: Choose an essay of this time period. Then, in an attempt to see how the author does his or her work, fill in the information.

Title and author ______________________________

Type of essay ______________________________

Purpose of essay ______________________________

OPINIONS IN ESSAY

1. ______________________________

____

2. ______________________________

SUPPORTING FACTS OR STATISTICS

1. ______________________________

____

2. ______________________________

____

3. ______________________________

____

DIRECTIONS: Now choose one sentence that especially typifies your author's style and copy it here.

____

____

____

____

Name ______________________________ Date ______________

4-17. 1 + 1 = 1

As the United States changed, so too did American English. The language adjusted to changes in its surroundings and to new ideas, products, and ways of doing things. All of these required new words. One way in which new words were produced was by forming *combinations* such as *bullfrog, sweet potato, jack rabbit,* and *redwood.*

DIRECTIONS: Think of word combinations that would fit each category below.

CATTLE RANCHING

1. ______________
2. ______________
3. ______________
4. ______________
5. ______________
6. ______________
7. ______________

THE ALL-AMERICAN GAME

1. ______________
2. ______________
3. ______________
4. ______________
5. ______________
6. ______________
7. ______________

NAMES BEGINNING WITH "NEW"

1. ______________
2. ______________
3. ______________
4. ______________
5. ______________
6. ______________
7. ______________

NAMES ENDING IN "VILLE"

1. ______________
2. ______________
3. ______________
4. ______________
5. ______________
6. ______________
7. ______________

4-18. VOCABULARY LIST

1. abashed
2. abide
3. alacrity
4. allay
5. anathema
6. antipathy
7. autocratic
8. averse
9. bane
10. bastion
11. brandish
12. capitulate
13. catechize
14. chafe
15. churlish
16. concentric
17. courier
18. covenant
19. demeanor
20. deprivation
21. diadem
22. didactic
23. discern
24. dissolute
25. dormant
26. elemental
27. emancipation
28. enfranchise
29. ephemeral
30. eradication
31. ethereal
32. exemplary
33. exhort
34. exude
35. fathom
36. foment
37. hoary
38. importune
39. incantation
40. incendiary
41. influx
42. inherent
43. irresolute
44. lattice
45. lintel
46. ludicrous
47. manifold
48. metamorphose
49. mutation
50. nonconformist
51. obsequious
52. opprobrium
53. penitent
54. philanthropy
55. placid
56. prerogative
57. reprove
58. sachem
59. scintillation
60. self-reliance
61. solitude
62. Spartan
63. squalor
64. stupendous
65. sublime
66. superficial
67. superfluous
68. titular
69. torpor
70. tumultuous
71. turbulent
72. uncouth
73. verdant
74. visage
75. zenith

Name ______________________ Date ______________

4-19. CROSSWORD

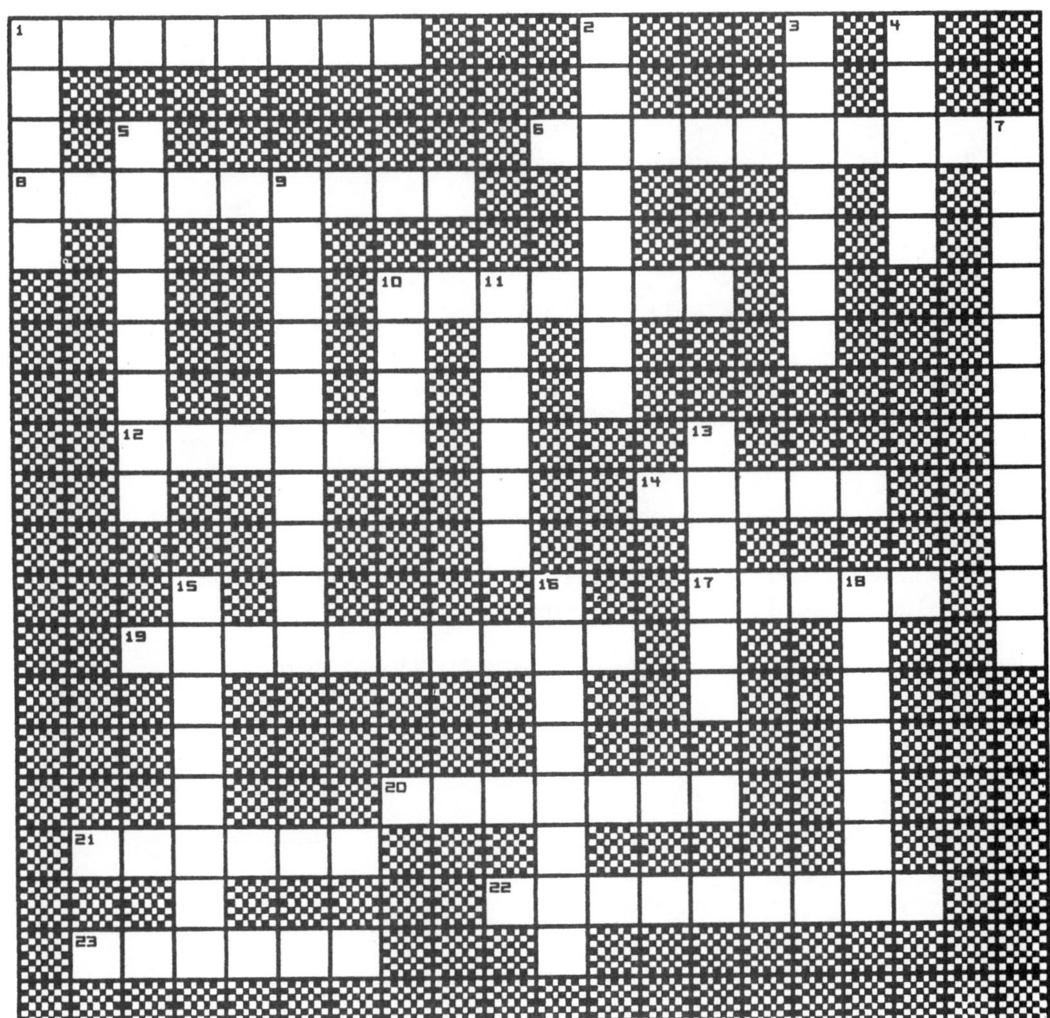

ACROSS

1. eagerness; lively action
6. to surrender
8. feeling of aversion
10. well-fortified position
12. opposed, reluctant
14. gray or white with age
17. to ooze forth
19. having a common center
20. to perceive or detect
21. crown
22. lacking in moral restraint
23. six feet

DOWN

1. to lessen or relieve
2. wave menacingly
3. messenger
4. irritate by rubbing
5. delicate, highly refined
7. annihilation
9. arrogant, domineering
10. cause of death, destruction
11. tribal chief
13. stir up, instigate
15. compact, contract
16. intended to instruct
18. not awake or active

Name ______________________________ Date ______________

4-20. CONCRETE AND ABSTRACT

A familiarity with types of words can help you write and speak with accuracy. A *concrete word* is one that refers to an actual, specific person, thing, or instance that can be perceived by the senses (i.e., seen, touched, felt, smelled, heard).

DIRECTIONS: List five concrete words from the vocabulary list.

CONCRETE WORDS

______________________ ______________________

______________________ ______________________

____

An *abstract word* refers to an idea, feeling, or quality that does not have a concrete existence. The meanings of many of these words are often unclear, and they can mean different things to different people. Examples of abstract words are *truth, jealousy, freedom.*

DIRECTIONS: List five abstract words from the vocabulary list.

ABSTRACT WORDS

______________________ ______________________

______________________ ______________________

____

DIRECTIONS: Now choose two words from each list and use them in a sentence in such a way that the meaning of the word is clear; that is, so that we can figure out the meaning from the context.

____

____

____

____

____

____

____

Name ______________________________ Date ______________

4-21. THINK IT THROUGH

Analogies

1. Ephemeral : Perpetual ::
   A. Forever: Eternal
   B. Day : Month
   C. Transitory : Everlasting
   D. Solitude : Quiet
   E. Cognizance : Understanding
2. Spartan : Scanty ::
   A. Athens : Classical
   B. Frugal : Spare
   C. Gaudy : Wealth
   D. Monastery : Solitude
   E. Placid : School
3. Visage : Nose ::
   A. Eye : Sight
   B. Fathom : Ship
   C. Storm : Hurricane
   D. Light : Dark
   E. Church : Altar
4. Stupendous : Nice ::
   A. Frigid : Chilly
   B. Lintel : Doorway
   C. Wonderful : Awful
   D. Brandish : Tarnish
   E. Rug : Carpet
5. Foment : Rebellion ::
   A. Chafe : Dish
   B. Exhort : Plead
   C. Light : Match
   D. Jump : Leap
   E. Deprive : Deprivation
6. Sachem : Tribe ::
   A. Buffalo : Hunt
   B. Settle : Frontier
   C. Nonconformist : Group
   D. General : Army
   E. Luck : Plan

Synonyms and Antonyms

You will find a synonym and antonym answer for each word below. Mark the synonyms with an S and the antonyms with an A.

1. Uncouth
   A. Courteous B. Fast C. Churlish D. Damp E. Passionate

2. Emancipation
   A. Union B. Enslavement C. War D. Employment E. Freedom

3. Antipathy
   A. Love B. Bravery C. Dislike D. Pathetic E. Spaghetti

4. Zenith
   A. Equator B. Enclosure C. Nadir D. Acme E. North Pole

5. Turbulent
   A. Propulsion B. Disorderly C. Sad D. Dirty E. Placid

Section 5

REALISM AND NATURALISM

1870-1917 Twain to Masters

SKILLS INDEX

Thinking Skills		Worksheet
Deductive reasoning	5-8	Authors Go Freud
	5-1	Get Real
	5-13	This Is Poetry?
	5-5	The Wounds Heal Slowly
Drawing conclusions	5-11	Follow Me
	5-4	Getting Out the News
	5-13	This Is Poetry?
Generalizing	5-15	A Rose Is a Rose—Or Is It?
	5-2	New Energies
	5-6	Out West
	5-12	Sounds Like . . .
Prioritizing	5-4	Getting Out the News
Synthesizing	5-15	A Rose Is a Rose—Or Is It?
	5-1	Get Real!
	5-14	Sensational!
	5-5	The Wounds Heal Slowly

Vocabulary Skills		Worksheet
Analogies, synonyms, antonyms	5-22	Think It Through
Connotation	5-20	What Are You Suggesting?
Denotation	5-20	What Are You Suggesting?
General and specific Words	5-21	Ran or Sprinted?
	5-19	Vocabulary List

Other Skills		Worksheet
Author biography	5-7	I've Been There

WORKSHEET NOTES

5-1. Get Real!

5-2. New Energies

5-3. Realism Squared

The first three worksheets of this section deal with author viewpoint, new philosophies, and new realities in American life. These worksheets make a good review after examples of the different styles have been read. The new viewpoints and styles of writing reflect events: the problems that come with growth and urbanization, the loss of the innocence and idealism of the past, among others. The exercises should help students see the reflection of society in literature and the relationship between literature and life. Students will see Whitman as a bridge between the romantics and the realists. They will also notice that the regionalists were realistic writers and that Crane and Bierce could only be naturalists.

5-4. Getting Out the News

It is helpful to have a daily newspaper in the room for this exercise. Students can then follow the format, including the placement and size of the articles, if they wish. They can also be encouraged to use a history book for information other than that found in the text's introduction to this time period. If the students work independently, it may be fun to compare priorities and headlines at the end of the hour.

5-5. The Wounds Heal Slowly

5-6. Out West

These two worksheets are related to worksheet 5-4; they concentrate on ideas and events that were probably considered for front-page placement. Students will probably see that all three problems they gleaned from the literature for the first of these exercises are still with us today. The five-paragraph expository composition is such a basic form that mastery of it is essential. In fact, some introductory college English classes are based on it. Topics likely to be included are mining, farming, relationships with native Americans, and transportation, especially railroads.

5-7. I've Been There

This should be a fairly easy exercise for literature students. In fact, they should be able to easily do twice the amount asked for by the exercise. The obvious point of the lesson should apply to student writing also: we write best about those things we know. Students can either stick with the familiar or learn something new, then write about it.

5-8. Authors Go Freud

Just as the United States was moving from innocence to maturity, so were many characters depicted in some of the great literature of the era. As more characters looked inward, readers became more aware of psychological motivation and self-discovery in works by such authors as Chopin, Crane, Bierce, Twain, and others. Students can watch a Henry Fleming and Huck Finn move to awareness and maturity. This understanding will help prepare them for the psychological realism of much twentieth-century literature. And if students can look inward with literary characters, maybe it will be easier for them to understand times of personal internal conflict. To do this exercise students must first realize that a character has a conflict with self; then they must know what the conflict is and continue to follow it to its resolution. Ask the students if they learned anything from the character's struggles. It might be pointed out that a moment of sudden awareness and understanding is called an *epiphany*.

5-9. Free – but Now What?

This exercise can be used with any group including Native Americans, women, and adolescents, with only slight changes in directions. It might be enlightening to do this worksheet with a second group to see the similarities and differences. The reading discernment and thought processes necessary to do the work are fairly mature. It is also good for students to understand the difference between paraphrasing and summarizing.

5-10. From Within

After looking into the minds of others in previous worksheets, students are asked to turn their attention to themselves and decide what happens when they read a poem. Poems, when read well, do speak to us; we do bring our thoughts, personalities, and experiences to the interpretation of poetry. In fact, the reading process is not really complete until we are aware of our reactions. If done spontaneously, some of the written ideas may surprise the students. It is fun to assess their reactions as they look over what they wrote.

5-11. Follow Me

This worksheet draws on themes studied previously and asks students to realize that the ideals of our founders are still part of American society, but they, too, have matured. We see in the literature of the era whole groups of people who have to fight for their equality. The exercise should also help students to see American history and literature as a continuing process. None of these great works occur in isolation. Like people, literature has a past and a future.

5-12. Sounds Like . . .

5-13. This Is Poetry?

5-14. Sensational!

5-15. A Rose Is a Rose – or Is It?

These four worksheets ask students to look at and understand how authors do their work and, in some cases, to try their hand at the techniques. If they have trouble understanding what a particular technique has added, they might reword the lines in question and note what is lost, such as compactness of language, emphasis of certain ideas, depth of meaning, and so on. All of the techniques covered are basic to a good understanding of literature in general.

5-16. Dickinson

5-17. Twain's Humor

It is often less frightening for a student to write an original poem while pretending to be someone else. But to do that, the student must have a good knowledge of that poet's work, including style, mood, subject matter, and typical techniques used. The question following the poem on the first worksheet returns students firmly to the present day and allows them to do some comparison and contrast thinking. The Twain worksheet also asks students to analyze style, in this case how Twain achieves his humor. Only the word *colloquialism* ("up and asked") should need explanation.

5-18. Here Lies

This exercise, while teaching a literary term, is basically just for fun, although the epitaphs may be serious. Students shouldn't have any trouble with it.

5-19. Vocabulary List

5-20. What Are You Suggesting?

5-21. Ran or Sprinted?

5-22. Think It Through

The vocabulary study adds additional information about the workings of the language. Denotation and connotation are basic ideas, as are general and specific words. The concepts are not difficult, but students need to be aware of the type of words they use and the effects of those words. The answers for Think It Through follow.

Answers

Analogies	Synonyms	Antonyms
1. B (synonyms)	1. E	C
2. E (degree of reaction)	2. C	A
3. A (small to large, D is backward)	3. B	D
4. D (degree, ostentatious to average)	4. A	E
5. C (antonyms)	5. C	B
6. B (synonymous in regard to color)		

PROJECT IDEAS

Contest

Have a jumping-frog-type contest, but use students instead of frogs. Determine contest rules and prizes. No buckshot allowed.

Photographs

Take snapshots around the community, school, and home that would serve to illustrate selections from this unit. Make a display for the class, labeling each snapshot appropriately.

Read Aloud

Several students read aloud works not in the text by poets being studied. The class then guesses who wrote each poem. Opinions should be supported by references to style and subject matter. The class can be divided into two teams and score can be kept. This project can also be used as a written assignment.

Research

Research the following for oral or written reports: the Atlantic cable, a gold rush, Mississippi steamboats, the Model T, Halley's comet, Appaloosa horses, Reconstruction, the Pulitzer Prize, life on a reservation, education, the telephone, alternating current, farm machinery, the X-ray, Tiffany glass, segregation, Oklahoma Territory, the buffalo, new millionaires, the beginnings of the National Association for the Advancement of Colored People, local events of the time.

Depict a Scene

Divide the class into small groups and have them depict a definitive scene from an author's life. Students may choose information from the biographical sketches in their textbooks or choose to do some research. Each group should write an original script for the performance; a narrator can set the scene.

Local Cemetery

Copy information from the tombstones of people who lived in your community during the period being studied. Note any unusual information, such as an unusual number of deaths at about the same time, or notable epitaphs. Rubbings with butcher paper and crayons can be shared with the rest of the class. (Check whether permission is necessary for rubbings).

News Items

Many libraries have newspapers or microfiche of newspapers from this time period. Copy some of these articles for a topical classroom display.

CHRONOLOGY

1870—Harte, *The Luck of Roaring Camp*

1871—Darwin, *The Descent of Man*

—Apache wars in New Mexico and Arizona begin

1872—Yellowstone National Park established

1874—Barbed wire patented

1875-1876—Second Sioux War led by Crazy Horse and Sitting Bull

1875—Civil Rights Act

—Black Hills of South Dakota opened to gold prospectors

1876—Colorado admitted to the Union

—Hayes elected president

—Telephone invented by Bell

—Twain, *The Adventures of Tom Sawyer*

1877—Nez Percé War

1878—Phonograph patented by Edison

1879—"Exodus" of twenty thousand to forty thousand ex-slaves to Kansas

—Incandescent bulb invented by Edison

1880—Harris, *Uncle Remus*

—Garfield elected president

1881—First Jim Crow law passed in Tennessee

—President Garfield assassinated, Arthur becomes president

1883—Twain, *Life on the Mississippi*

—Time zones established in the United States

1884—Jewett, *A Country Doctor*

—Twain, *The Adventures of Huckleberry Finn*

—Cleveland elected president

1886—American Federation of Labor founded

1887—U.S. naval base established at Pearl Harbor

1888—Harrison elected president

1890—Bierce, *An Occurrence at Owl Creek Bridge*

—Massacre at Wounded Knee

—Oklahoma Territory organized

—Dickinson, *Poems*

1891—Wilkins, *A New England Nun*

—International Copyright Act

1892—Cleveland elected president

1895—Crane, *The Red Badge of Courage*

1896—McKinley elected president

—Klondike Gold Rush

1898—Spanish-American War

—Puerto Rico and Guam ceded to the United States; Hawaii annexed

1899—Gold discovered in Alaska

1900—McKinley reelected

—Eight thousand cars registered in the United States

1901—B. T. Washington, *Up from Slavery*

1902—Bret Harte dies

1903—Wright brothers' flight at Kittyhawk

—United States granted perpetual control of the Panama Canal

1904—Roosevelt elected president

1905—Niagara Conference held, headed by W.E.B. Du Bois

1907—Oklahoma admitted to the Union

1908—Taft elected president

—Model T designed by Ford

1909—National Association for the Advancement of Colored People (NAACP) founded

1910—Mark Twain dies; Halley's Comet returns

1912—Wilson elected president

—Arizona admitted to the Union

1914—World War I begins

1915—*Lusitania* sunk by Germany

1916—Submachine gun invented by Thompson

1917—United States enters World War I

BIBLIOGRAPHY

Andrist, Ralph K., ed. *The American Heritage History of the Confident Years.* New York: American Heritage Publishing, 1969.

Bird, Isabella. *A Lady's Life in the Rocky Mountains.* Sausalito, CA: Comstock Editions, 1987.

Brown, Dee. *Bury My Heart at Wounded Knee: An Indian History of the American West.* Orlando, FL: Holt, Rinehart and Winston, 1970.

Cady, Edwin H. *Stephen Crane.* Boston: G. K. Hall, 1980.

Chopin, Kate. *The Awakening.* New York: Avon, 1972.

DeVoto, Bernard. *Across the Wide Missouri.* Boston: Houghton Mifflin, 1964.

Hill, Ruth Beebe. *Hanto Yo.* New York: Doubleday, 1979.

Horgan, Paul. *Lamy of Santa Fe.* New York: Farrar, Straus, and Giroux, 1975.

Johnson, R. P. *Chief Joseph.* Minneapolis, MN: Dillon, 1974.

Kaplan, Justin. *Mr. Clemens and Mark Twain.* New York: Simon and Schuster, 1983.

Lomax, Alan. *The Folk Songs of North America.* New York: Doubleday, 1960.

Massey, John K. *The Comic Spirit in America.* New York: Scribner's, 1969.

Rolvaag, O. E. *Giants in the Earth.* New York: Harper and Row, 1955.

Schultz, James Willard. *My Life as an Indian.* New York: Beaufort Book, 1968.

Simon, Myron. *Ethnic Writers in America.* San Diego, CA: Harcourt Brace, Jovanovich, 1972.

Snelling, William Joseph. *Tales of the Northwest.* New York: Dorset Press, 1985.

Stone, Irving. *Men to Match My Mountains.* New York: Doubleday, 1956.

Wolff, Cynthia Griffin. *Emily Dickinson.* New York: Knopf, 1987.

Name ______________________________ Date ______________

5-1. GET REAL!

Realism dominated American literature during this period. Romanticism was considered too idealized to reflect the new postwar society. Realism tried to show life exactly as it was lived and events exactly as they occurred, as journalistic writing proposed to do. In realistic literature the protagonist is usually an ordinary person living an ordinary life. These protagonists could exhibit heroism but were not the classic heroes of the past. The modern American problems of sweatshops, labor strife, urban poverty, "robber barons," corrupt politicians, and crime were born during this era.

DIRECTIONS: Choose two authors who you feel wrote realistically. Explain how the subject matter and the protagonists fit this category.

Author 1 ______________________________

Title ______________________________

Subject matter ______________________________

____

____

____

____

Protagonist ______________________________

____

Author 2 ______________________________

Title ______________________________

Subject matter ______________________________

____

____

____

____

Protagonist ______________________________

____

Name ______________________ Date ______________

5-2. NEW ENERGIES

During this period in American literature, many authors brought into the language the dialects, habits of thought, and mannerisms of the language of river boatmen, farmers, miners, and others. A subdivision of *realism,* but not as serious, *local color* used language that was native to a region; it was often slangy. Local color is a form of *regionalism,* that is, literature that arises from a particular geographic region and that includes not only language usage particular to a certain area but the history, beliefs, dress, and topography of the area. In American literature, Harte, Twain, Murfree, Harris, Jewett, Freeman, Chopin, and others are examples of regional or local-color writers.

DIRECTIONS: Quote two sentences that are examples of local color from literature of each of the following areas.

NEW ENGLAND

1. ______________________________

____

2. ______________________________

____

THE SOUTH

1. ______________________________

____

2. ______________________________

____

THE WEST

1. ______________________________

____

2. ______________________________

____

DIRECTIONS: Choose one of these quotes and rewrite it into "proper" English. Which way of writing the sentence is better for the story? Why?

Name ______________________________ Date ______________

5-3. REALISM SQUARED

As the works of Newton, Darwin, Freud, Comte, and Zola became known, some American literature began to portray a new philosophy, called *naturalism,* based on scientific determinism. Science had shown that people are part of nature and subject to its laws. Environment and heredity determine our characters and our fate, and we can control neither. Whereas the realists felt we lived in a moral universe, the universe of the naturalists had no spirit; it was aloof. Naturalists saw life as dark and often depict disillusioned people in machinelike terms. This way of looking at the universe would gain momentum, reaching its culmination in the middle of the next century.

DIRECTIONS: Choose two works of literature from this period of study, one by a romantic or realist and one by a naturalist. Show how they differ in the following categories.

ROMANTIC OR REALIST	NATURALIST
Depiction of people	
Attitude toward nature	
Outlook for the future	
Subject matter	
Tone	

Name ______________________________ Date ______________

5-4. GETTING OUT THE NEWS

It is the second half of the nineteenth century and you are putting together the front page of the morning edition of a newspaper, one much like you read today. It is nearing the time to put the paper to bed and you must decide what is front-page news. It is a difficult task because so much is happening: immigrants arriving by the thousands, Reconstruction, problems with Native Americans, new inventions, the new problem of urban poverty, and so much more.

DIRECTIONS: Below, write in the name, location, and date of the newspaper. Sketch in the placement and size of the news stories. Then, write the headline and first sentence for each. Be sure to include the five W's: who, what, where, when, why.

Name ______________________________ Date ______________

5-5. THE WOUNDS HEAL SLOWLY

The Civil War and the events associated with it were still a very real part of the lives of the people during this time. Many authors either wrote about these events directly or alluded to them in prose and poetry. The wounds left by the war, internal and external, were healing very slowly. In fact, many feel that those wounds are not yet healed.

DIRECTIONS: Choose three authors who wrote of events concerning the Civil War and determine the main problems left from the war. Fill in the chart.

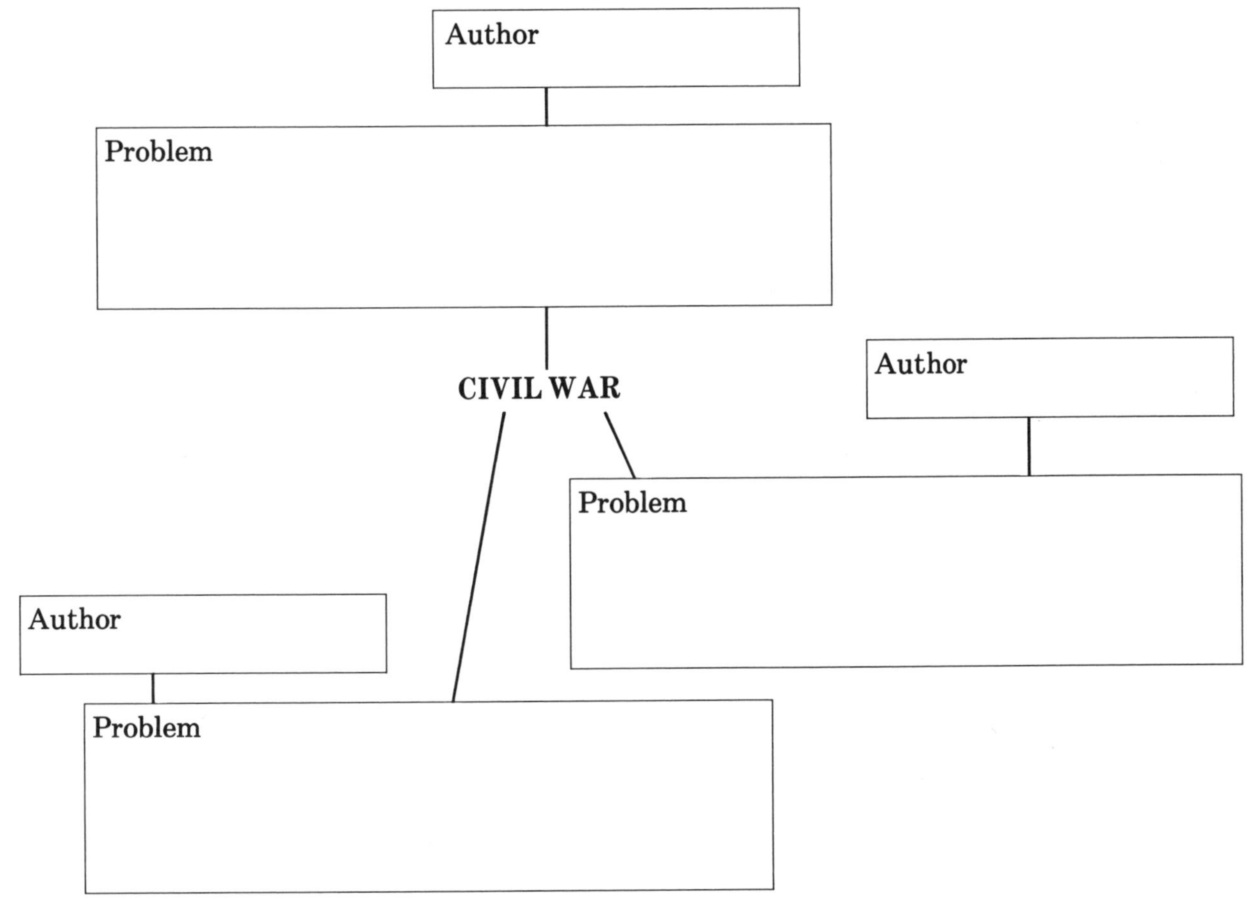

DIRECTIONS: Choose one of the problems from your chart and tell how it is still part of today's social fabric.

____

____

____

____

Name ______________________________ Date ______________

5-6. OUT WEST

Much was happening in the American West during this period, events that laid the foundation for the twentieth century for the people who followed. Using the literature of this time period, tell what it was like "out there" by writing an essay describing events and the people involved in them. The following pattern shows one way to set up your paper:

I. Thesis statement

II. Paragraphs 1 through 3—each includes one event and the people involved

III. Conclusion—a restatement of the thesis and a summing up of your paper

DIRECTIONS: Use this page to put together your preliminary ideas. On another piece of paper, write the rough draft, keeping in mind that you need clear transitions to connect your paragraphs. The final copy will be done in ink or typed on unlined paper.

EVENT	PEOPLE INVOLVED	LOCATION
1.		
2.		
3.		

Name ______________________________ Date ______________

5-7. I'VE BEEN THERE

Authors are usually most comfortable writing about what they know and, often, have experienced. That is why so many great works have such an aura of authenticity and immediacy. In fact, you can often trace much of the author's biography in his or her writing.

DIRECTIONS: Try it. Study a biographical sketch of one author. Then, match five events or ideas from that life with the writings. For example, Mark Twain was raised in a small town in Missouri located on the Mississippi River. Tom Sawyer, one of Twain's most famous characters, lived in a small Missouri town on the Mississippi River.

AUTHOR (from the biography)	LITERATURE (from the writings)
1. ______________________________	1. ______________________________
______________________________	______________________________
______________________________	______________________________
2. ______________________________	2. ______________________________
______________________________	______________________________
______________________________	______________________________
3. ______________________________	3. ______________________________
______________________________	______________________________
______________________________	______________________________
4. ______________________________	4. ______________________________
______________________________	______________________________
______________________________	______________________________
5. ______________________________	5. ______________________________
______________________________	______________________________
______________________________	______________________________

Name ______________________________ Date ______________

5-8. AUTHORS GO FREUD

Several authors of this era were precursors of the psychological realism so prevalent in the twentieth century. We see more internal conflict, more introspection, more concern with self-discovery in their works. A major character will move from innocence to maturity. Interior action and motives, although always present, gained more prominence.

DIRECTIONS: Choose one character who experienced internal conflict (person vs. self) and fill in the information.

Name of character ______________________________

Author of work ______________________________

Title of work ______________________________

Basic internal conflict ______________________________

____

____

____

Moment of most intense conflict ______________________________

____

____

Result (What was learned? How did the person change?) ______________________________

____

____

____

____

____

____

____

____

____

____

Name ______________________ Date ____________

5-9. FREE—BUT NOW WHAT?

One very significant aspect of the Civil War was Emancipation. Using the literature of this era, it is possible to discern much about the lives of ex-slaves.

DIRECTIONS: Choose two examples of literature by African-Americans of the era. Briefly describe those lives from the author's point of view, quoting descriptive words and phrases to illustrate the ideas. Note attitudes and tones.

Author 1 ______________________

Title(s) ______________________

Life as depicted by the author ______________________

Author 2 ______________________

Title(s) ______________________

Life as depicted by the author ______________________

Name ______________________ Date ______________

5-10. FROM WITHIN

DIRECTIONS: Read again a poem from this era of American literature. Then put your pen on the top line below and write anything that comes to your mind concerning the poem. Tell how the poem makes you feel and what thoughts arise. Do not lift your pen from the paper until you reach the end; keep writing without worrying about sentence structure, spelling, punctuation, or even logic. When you are finished, look over the results and note (1) those reactions that came directly from the poem and (2) those that contained elements of your own emotions and experiences. Number them (1) or (2) accordingly.

Title and author ______________________

Name ______________________________ Date ______________

5-11. FOLLOW ME

As you read the literature of this era, you will notice most of the themes that have been present in American literature from the beginning. You may see a new point of view, but authors are still concerned with such ideas as equality, democracy, self-reliance, rugged individualism, religion and God, and love. Making a relatively new appearance are the concentrations on war, death, poverty, injustice, and the "common" people.

DIRECTIONS: Choose one theme and follow it through American literature. Select from each of three periods one work of literature containing the theme you chose. (You may use literature from the twentieth century for one period.) Summarize below the point of view of each author (i.e., what seems to be the author's attitude concerning this theme?).

Theme ______________________________

Period 1 ______________________________

Title ______________________________ Author ______________

Summary ______________________________

____

____

____

Period 2 ______________________________

Title ______________________________ Author ______________

Summary ______________________________

____

____

____

Period 3 ______________________________

Title ______________________________ Author ______________

Summary ______________________________

____

____

____

Name ______________________________ Date ______________

5-12. SOUNDS LIKE . . .

Alliteration is the repetition of initial or beginning consonant sounds, as in the phrase "*b*right *b*lue *b*laze of the noon sun." This technique is often used to draw attention to an object or an idea and to add to the rhythm of the poem. *Assonance* is the repetition of vowel sounds in stressed syllables to achieve partial rhyme, as in the phrase "br*a*ve l*a*dies live not in v*a*in."

DIRECTIONS: Find four examples of alliteration and assonance from the poetry of the era and place them in the correct places below. Then write two original examples of each technique.

ALLITERATION	ASSONANCE
1. ______________________________	1. ______________________________
______________________________	______________________________
2. ______________________________	2. ______________________________
______________________________	______________________________
3. ______________________________	3. ______________________________
______________________________	______________________________
4. ______________________________	4. ______________________________
______________________________	______________________________
5. ______________________________	5. ______________________________
______________________________	______________________________
6. ______________________________	6. ______________________________
______________________________	______________________________

DIRECTIONS: Choose one example from your list and explain what the technique added to the poem.

____

____

____

____

____

Name ______________________________ Date ______________

5-13. THIS IS POETRY?

Free verse is poetry that does not have a regular meter or a conventional stanza pattern. If the poem has rhyme, the rhyme scheme will be irregular.

DIRECTIONS: From the literature of this era choose a stanza of poetry that appears to be free verse. Copy it below. Then prove that your choice was correct by scanning the meter and attempting to determine a rhyme scheme.

Title of poem ______________________________

____

____

____

____

____

____

____

____

____

Free verse, can be very rhythmical, however. It can achieve rhythm with such techniques as cadence, alliteration, parallel constructions, and line length. Below, show if any of these techniques were used in the passage you chose.

Cadence

Alliteration

Parallel syntax

Similarity of line length

Name ______________________________ Date ______________

5-14. SENSATIONAL!

A poet uses figures of speech to create mental pictures or images in the mind of the reader. Often the poet will use vivid descriptive words that appeal to our senses—sight, sound, taste, touch, smell—to make a scene come alive. This technique, in which the author uses *sensory imagery,* helps us to actually experience a poem. For example, if an evening is so humid that the air is "palpable," the author is appealing to our sense of touch as well as giving us a vivid image of the degree of humidity and, at the same time, connoting a certain unpleasantness.

DIRECTIONS: Choose five passages from poetry of the era that expressly appeal to our senses. Label each according to the sense involved. Aim for a variety.

1. Title and author ______________________________

   Passage ______________________________

   ____

   ____

2. Title and author ______________________________

   Passage ______________________________

   ____

   ____

3. Title and author ______________________________

   Passage ______________________________

   ____

   ____

4. Title and author ______________________________

   Passage ______________________________

   ____

   ____

5. Title and author ______________________________

   Passage ______________________________

   ____

   ____

Name ______________________ Date ______________

5-15. A ROSE IS A ROSE—OR IS IT?

A *symbol* is an object or event that signifies something else; in other words, a symbol is itself but also means something more. For example, the American flag symbolizes our country and everything for which it stands. A rose often symbolizes love; a dove can symbolize peace.

DIRECTIONS: Find two symbols found in the writing of two authors of this era and fill in the chart below.

AUTHOR #1	AUTHOR #2
Title	
Symbol	
Symbolic meaning	

DIRECTIONS: We are surrounded by symbols. Choose one that you see often in magazines or newspapers or on television. Then do the following:

1. Describe the symbol.

2. Explain the symbolic meaning.

3. Explain why the symbol is or is not a good one to accomplish its purpose.

Name ______________________________ Date ________________

5-16. DICKINSON

Emily Dickinson wrote poems about things that were part of her life. In her own inimitable style, she made ordinary objects and creatures seem real and important.

DIRECTIONS: Using Emily Dickinson's style of writing, compose a poem about something that is a normal part of your everyday life. Possible subjects might be a fly at the window, a bird flying across the sky or perched in a tree, a dog barking, a howling coyote, or a startled mouse. Be certain to use exact, vivid images. Try to use a metaphor or simile in your poem.

Title ______________________________

DIRECTIONS: Explain to a young student what your poem is about and tell that novice to poetry what techniques you used to achieve the finished product.

Name ______________________________ Date ______________

5-17. TWAIN'S HUMOR

Samuel Clemens, alias Mark Twain, achieved his humor in various ways. Irony, colloquialism, exaggeration, strange occurrences, and personality quirks were all part of his arsenal of humor. Twain also made use of what he called *finesse,* a trick through which the protagonist gets the upper hand.

DIRECTIONS: Find one example of each of the following in his writings.

1. irony ______________________________

____

____

2. colloquialism ______________________________

____

____

3. exaggeration ______________________________

____

____

4. strange occurrences ______________________________

____

____

5. personality quirk ______________________________

____

____

6. finesse ______________________________

____

____

On the back of this paper, tell of a time when you used finesse. Surely your parents or brothers and sisters have been involved.

Name ______________________________ Date ______________

5-18. HERE LIES

Usually found on tombstones, the *epitaph* is a brief comment, sometimes in poetry, about a dead person or about life or death. Epitaphs have been featured on tombstones since the colonial period and can be found well into the twentieth century. Edgar Lee Masters wrote longer epitaphs for the citizens of his fictitious Spoon River.

DIRECTIONS: Fill in the names, dates, and an appropriate epitaph below. Choose two people from literature, a real well-known person, or a fictitious person; for example, Here Lies Prissy Perky, Housekeeper, 1682–1740, "Excuse My Dust."

5-19. VOCABULARY LIST

1. adroit
2. apprise
3. aromatic
4. ascetic
5. bayou
6. bellicose
7. choleric
8. cloister
9. conjecture
10. copious
11. coquetry
12. cornice
13. courageous
14. debris
15. decorum
16. diadem
17. docile
18. dogmatic
19. doleful
20. efface
21. effuse
22. exhort
23. façade
24. forecastle
25. gamin
26. garrulous
27. grapple
28. guidon
29. impose
30. interpose
31. knell
32. languor
33. ludicrous
34. malevolence
35. maudlin
36. melee
37. molten
38. myriad
39. orb
40. ostracism
41. pantaloons
42. pariah
43. pathos
44. perilous
45. plaintive
46. prismatic
47. prodigious
48. proffer
49. pummel
50. respite
51. restive
52. reverie
53. roseate
54. rueful
55. sallow
56. sardonic
57. savant
58. sententious
59. sexton
60. sinuous
61. suffuse
62. surmount
63. surplice
64. sylvan
65. tableau
66. tedious
67. travail
68. undulate
69. vanquish
70. venerable
71. vexation
72. visage
73. vociferation
74. wend
75. yokel

Name ______________________________ Date ______________

5-20. WHAT ARE YOU SUGGESTING?

The *denotation* of a word is its explicit meaning; that is, its direct, precise meaning. The *connotation* of a word is a secondary meaning suggested by the word, especially feelings, negative or positive, that are brought to mind. For example, the denotative meanings of the words *economical* and *miserly* are synonymous. However, the connotative meanings are not. *Economical* carries a positive meaning, while *miserly* has a negative feeling about it.

DIRECTIONS: Choose ten words from the vocabulary list that carry connotative meanings and place them in the correct column below. Then, write a word with the same denotative meaning but an opposite connotative meaning.

POSITIVE	NEGATIVE
1. ________________	1. ________________
2. ________________	2. ________________
3. ________________	3. ________________
4. ________________	4. ________________
5. ________________	5. ________________
6. ________________	6. ________________
7. ________________	7. ________________
8. ________________	8. ________________
9. ________________	9. ________________
10. ________________	10. ________________

DIRECTIONS: Write a pair of sentences. In the first, use a word from one of the columns above; in the second, use the companion word in the opposite column. Notice what emotional changes occur in the second sentence.

1. ____

____

2. ____

____

Name ______________________________ Date ______________

5-21. RAN OR SPRINTED?

The authors of the selections in this unit chose their words with care so that their descriptions and ideas would be clear and concise. A reader cannot "see" in his or her mind clearly if an author does not choose words that are specific. This is not to say that it is incorrect to use general words; it is to say that a writer or speaker needs to be aware of the difference. For example, *card game* is general, *canasta* is specific; *ran* is general, *sprinted* is specific; *instrument* is general, *oboe* is specific.

DIRECTIONS: Choose three general words from the vocabulary list for each category below, then write a more specific one for each. Do the opposite for Part II.

I. GENERAL	SPECIFIC
1. ______________	1. ______________
2. ______________	2. ______________
3. ______________	3. ______________
II. SPECIFIC	**GENERAL**
1. ______________	1. ______________
2. ______________	2. ______________
3. ______________	3. ______________

DIRECTIONS: Write a descriptive paragraph five to six sentences long, perhaps of something you can see now or of a scene that you know well. Use very general words. Then rewrite the paragraph on the back of this page using very specific words.

____

____

____

____

____

____

____

____

Name ________________________________ Date ______________

5-22. THINK IT THROUGH

Analogies

1. Adroit : Adept ::
   A. Clever : Cleave
   B. Tedious : Tiresome
   C. Intelligent : Average
   D. Courageous : Cowardly
   E. Diligent : Devout
2. Maudlin : Sad ::
   A. Docile : Obedient
   B. Happy : Plaintive
   C. Languor : Loudness
   D. Sad : Mad
   E. Violent : Vexed
3. Stream : Bayou ::
   A. Cottage : Mansion
   B. Ocean : Continent
   C. Dog : Cat
   D. Rock : Pebble
   E. Homework : Desk
4. Diadem : Cap ::
   A. Beret : Hat
   B. Queen : King
   C. Orb : Sun
   D. Mansion : Cottage
   E. Pantaloons : Shirt
5. Knell : Peal ::
   A. Vanquish : Subjugate
   B. Surplice : Cassock
   C. Gloom : Joy
   D. Visage : Face
   E. Melee : Chaos
6. Roseate : Rosy ::
   A. Choleric : Happy
   B. Sallow : Yellow
   C. Purple : Green
   D. Hat : Cap
   E. Visage : Usage

Synonyms and Antonyms

You will find a synonym and an antonym answer for each word below. Mark the synonyms with an S and the antonyms with an A.

1. Molten
   A. Cool B. Lava C. Solid D. Volcano E. Liquid
2. Sylvan
   A. Urban B. Desert C. Forested D. Dreary E. Curtained
3. Savant
   A. Adolescent B. Scholar C. Priest D. Yokel E. Writer
4. Prodigious
   A. Enormous B. Successful C. Married D. Sallow E. Miniscule
5. Respite
   A. Hatred B. Hurry C. Rest D. Love E. Maudlin

Section 6
SOCIAL CHANGE

1917-1945 Sandburg to Wright

SKILLS INDEX

	6–11	"The Woods Are Lovely . . . "
Deductive reasoning	6–14	That Reminds Me
	6–7	"The True Essence of Civilization"
	6–5	Women in Literature
Drawing conclusions	6–10	American Humor
	6–3	Down on the Farm
	6–13	It's Not What You Say . . .
	6–4	The South Rises
	6–5	Women in Literature
Generalizing	6–9	Alienation
	6–15	My Hero!
	6–1	The Frontier
	6–4	The South Rises
Synthesizing	6–8	About Town Tonight
	6–2	The Dream Crashes
	6–1	The Frontier
	6–4	The South Rises

Vocabulary Skills		Worksheet
Analogies, synonyms, antonyms	6–22	Think It Through
Definition and meaning	6–21	Crossword
Formal English	6–20	Fit for the Occasion
Informal English	6–20	Fit for the Occasion

Other Skills		Worksheet
Role playing	6–5	Women in Literature
Social protest	6–6	I Object

WORKSHEET NOTES

6-1. The Frontier

6-2. The Dream Crashes

The first two worksheets ask students to understand the effects of two social phenomena as depicted in the literature of the time. For the first exercise, students can find frontier characters in the works of Faulkner, Cather, London, and others. The idea that the frontier is still with us is present in western novels and films, and stories set in the wilderness. Space exploration and medical research provide us with bona fide frontiers. It might be interesting to ask students to compare the characteristics of early frontier characters with those of our astronauts. Fitzgerald and Steinbeck could be used for the second worksheet. Jazz Age characters are often in pursuit of wealth, fame, and ideal love, looking outward rather than inward, spiritually dead. After Black Monday, when so many people lost not only material wealth but optimism, we see more characters who are devastated, in poverty and pain, looking inward for strength and understanding, often turning to the spiritual. There are fewer chances for individual wealth, more feelings of hopelessness. The lives of two well-chosen characters should show these differences.

6-3. Down on the Farm

The change of location of a character in literature often symbolizes a growth, a passage from innocence to experience, not only for the person but for the nation as well. Cather, Anderson, and Fitzgerald were some of the authors who depicted these changes. Remind students of the theme of initiation from the preceding chapter. They may notice that these characters gave up a closeness to nature, an understanding of the earth, for culture, exciting sounding jobs, new people. They suffer trials and hardships in the process, thereby gaining patience, a new maturity, and understanding of themselves and others.

6-4. The South Rises

This exercise reviews certain basic literary ideas as it draws attention to the great body of southern literature by both white and African-American authors, a phenomenon continuing to this day. Even though many of these authors depicted people at less than their best, the authors also depicted the people enduring. At first glance, the characters' view is pessimistic; a closer look shows this is not necessarily true. Somehow, these people, no matter what their handicaps are, make it and go on.

6-5. Women in Literature

For the most part, female stereotypes prevail in the literature written by men during this time. In fact, female characters are often in the background, and we get to know them only superficially. While not raging feminists in the works of female authors, women are usually depicted as thoughtful, making decisions, and, often, in control, even while living the same lives depicted in other works. They, too, have dreams, disappointments, and successes. They, too, go through transitions, learning and growing as time passes. Students should see more depth in the female characters of women authors.

6-6. I Object

Steinbeck, Langston Hughes and Alice Walker are only a few of those descended from a long line of authors who used their writing to address injustice. This exercise should help students see that the protesters of today are direct descendants of those who came to this country to build a better society. The authors of the Declaration of Independence and the Constitution would recognize these protesters as kindred spirits who had the right to express their ideas.

6-7. "The True Essence of Civilization"

The quiet understatement of the quotation provides a contrast to the styles of other authors of the era. A bit of this philosophy can be found in Frost, Faulkner, and Stuart, yet the emphasis is different. It is interesting to see students' reactions to Chief Standing Bear's philosophy.

6-8. About Town Tonight

This is one of a continuing series of worksheets that asks students to write newspaper articles. In fact, Sandburg and Frost drew large crowds when they came to town to read their poetry, especially Sandburg with his guitar. So this is a very logical article for the Arts and Events section of the newspaper.

6-9. Alienation

Wars, depression, government scandals, the rise of fascism, soup lines, unemployment, religious skepticism, industrial dehumanization, and urban crime are some of what shattered America's innate sense of optimism and the feeling that anything was possible. Once again, literature reflected society, and we see characters trying to face life with courage despite shattered dreams. It might be an interesting experiment to have students name the ten most momentous happenings in the twentieth century. Chances are they will think of wars and assassinations before they list the exciting advances in science and space travel and the fact that we have been blessed with some truly inspired leaders in many fields. If this is so, the students may yet be carrying the twentieth century spirit of pessimism. Students can be asked to name a literary character that best fits their way of looking at life.

6-10. American Humor

The two humorists examined here have much in common; for example, use of antiheroes (Mitty, Finn); regional in nature; piercing, devastating wit; psychological insight into people; irony; depiction of people trying to find their way in the world; a fondness for their characters. This look into characterization should allow students to see that, even though they are depicted humorously, people find their own ways to handle the events of their lives, no matter what the age in which they live. A good author shows us this and allows us to learn from these characters.

6-11. "The Woods Are Lovely . . ."

The ability to use language compactly, maximizing the use of every word, does not come easily to students. This exercise will allow them to practice this skill and, perhaps, appreciate the talent of a master.

6-12. Good Grief! Now Where?!

Much great twentieth-century fiction is difficult for students until they adjust to the heavy use of flashback by certain authors. This worksheet appears deceptively easy; it requires a careful reading of an entire story to be certain that events are in correct chronological order. Works by Eliot and Porter would also work here.

6-13. It's Not What You Say . . .

Words such as *technical, formal, informal, ornate, direct, dignified, elaborate, spare, intricate, abstract,* and *concrete* could appear on this worksheet. In fact, if students are having problems describing style, the teacher could put these words or others on the blackboard. The expository composition uses the basic comparison and contrast technique, one every student should have in his or her writing arsenal.

6-14. That Reminds Me

Stream of consciousness can be fun for students once they get a handle on it. This exercise will help them do that. Teachers might suggest that students try this technique themselves. Direct them to think of a subject, such as school, then for five minutes write down every thought that comes into their heads. No consideration should be given to correct grammar or spelling at this time—just be aware and write. The product could be very interesting.

6-15. My Hero!

Chances are, the anti-hero will be the one that comes closer to the students' lives, so they should be able to grasp the concept fairly easily. Fitzgerald and Thurber are two prominent authors who used the anti-hero in their works, but there are many others.

6-16. Speak to Me in Iambic

6-17. The Prairie Slumbers

These two worksheets give students the opportunity to work with three common poetic techniques. If necessary, teachers might want to use, for review purposes, the exercise from Section 2 concerning iambic pentameter and the one about scansion from Section 5. Poems by Sandburg, Frost, Eliot, and others contain good examples of personification and apostrophe.

6-18. Follow the Image

The concept of imagism is often difficult for students. However, looking carefully at one poem and noticing the careful word choice in the description of one object should help them understand the concept. It might be interesting to choose a poem by Emily Dickinson and debate whether she was our first imagist.

6-19. Vocabulary List

6-20. Fit for the Occasion

6-21. Crossword

6-22. Think It Through

The vocabulary section of this chapter is comprised of four worksheets. The worksheet concerning formal, informal, and substandard English makes a couple of important points. One is that because "it's in the dictionary" does not necessarily mean it is okay to say it any place, any time. Second, formal English should be mastered and used so that it becomes natural to use it on those very important occasions when we need it. The crossword puzzle is for fun, although it does bring important thinking skills into use.

Answers

Crossword

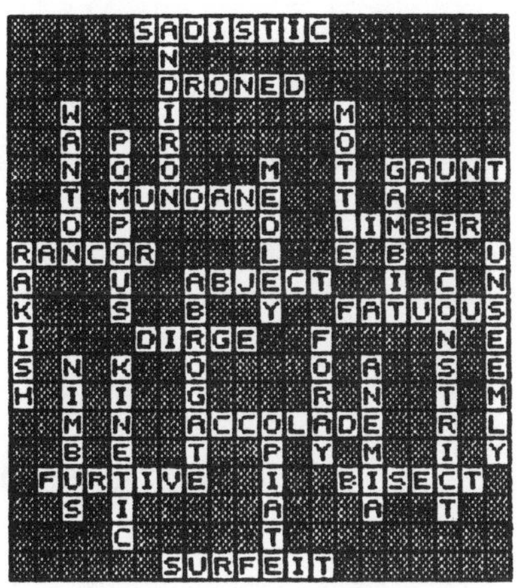

Think It Through

Analogies	Synonyms	Antonyms
1. B (opposites)	1. C	E
2. D (synonyms)	2. D	B
3. A (part of)	3. A	C
4. D (same suffixes)	4. E	B
5. C (place of activity)	5. E	B
6. E (condition of)		

PROJECT IDEAS

Public Service Announcement

Have a group of students do a sixty-second public service announcement concerning a prevailing social problem of the first half of the twentieth century. This should be videotaped and presented to the class. In fact, the entire class could be divided into four groups with each group doing its own announcement. Area television stations often have people who are willing to come into the classroom to share their expertise.

Learn a Dance

Several students could learn a dance from the era, such as the Charleston, and teach it to the rest of the class. Or, an outside person could teach the whole class.

Guest Speakers

Two or three students can work together to line up two or three classroom guests who have lived through some of the events of the era being studied. They could tell stories about the Depression, World War II, and jobs of the times. The class could prepare questions in advance.

Classroom Display

Transportation can be the subject of an interesting classroom display. Pictures, posters, and models of automobiles, trains, and airplanes of the era are readily available. The students who assemble the display can give a talk to the class concerning the items they brought and the state of transportation. This display could be added to as the second half of the twentieth century is studied.

Research

Research the following for oral or written reports: the Jazz Age, Freud, the *Saturday Evening Post,* the stock market crash, the Great Depression, Franklin Roosevelt's new government programs, any battle from World War II, Harlem, the expatriots, Henry Ford, the Pulitzer Prize, Sacco and Vanzetti, Charles Lindbergh, the Sioux Indian sun dance, women officeholders, or any item from the chronology.

Bring Music

Much music of the era remains available, from the jazz of the twenties to the ballads of the Depression to the songs of World War II. Several students could gather and play this music for the class.

CHRONOLOGY

1917—United States declares war on Germany

1918—Armistice is signed ending World War I

1919—Anderson, *Winesburg, Ohio*

1920—Harding elected president

—Women's suffrage

—First radio broadcast

—Lewis, *Main Street*

1922—Eliot, *The Waste Land*

1923—Ku Klux Klan revived at Stone Mountain, Georgia

—Harding dies; Coolidge becomes president

1924—Coolidge reelected

1925—Scopes and "Billy" Mitchell trials

—The *New Yorker* founded

—Fitzgerald, *The Great Gatsby*

1926—Hemingway, *The Sun also Rises*

1927—Lindbergh's solo flight—New York to Paris

—*The Jazz Singer*—first "talkie"

1928—Hoover elected president

1929—Stock Market Crash—the Great Depression begins

—Faulkner, *The Sound and the Fury*

—Wolfe, *Look Homeward, Angel*

—Hemingway, *A Farewell to Arms*

1931—Buck, *The Good Earth*

1932—Franklin Roosevelt elected president

1933—Twentieth and Twenty-first Amendments to the Constitution

1936—Dos Passos, *USA*

—Roosevelt reelected

—O'Neill wins Nobel Prize

1938—Buck receives Nobel Prize

—Wilder, *Our Town*

1939-1945—World War II

1939—Television

—Germany invades Poland; World War II begins

—Steinbeck, *The Grapes of Wrath*

—Hellman, *The Little Foxes*

—*The Wizard of Oz*—movie

—*Gone with the Wind*—movie

—Marian Anderson's concert at the Lincoln Memorial

1940—*The Great Dictator*—Charlie Chaplin movie

—*Fantasia*—Disney movie

—Germany invades Norway, the Netherlands, Belgium, Rumania, Luxembourg, France; the bombing of Britain begins

—Wright, *Native Son*

—Roosevelt reelected

—Faulkner, *The Hamlet*

—G. W. Carver establishes the Carver Foundation

1941—Sherwood Anderson dies

—Germany invades Greece, Yugoslavia, Soviet Union

—Japan attacks Pearl Harbor;

—U.S. enters World War II

1942—Japan shells parts of Alaska, Oregon, California

—Battles of Guadalcanal, Coral Sea, Midway

—U.S. forces land in Africa

—Forced relocation of Japanese Americans

—Congress of Racial Equality founded by James Farmer

1943—Germans forced from Soviet Union; Anglo-American army invades Sicily

—Race riots in Detroit, Mobile, and Harlem

1944—Williams, *The Glass Menagerie*

—D-Day

—Roosevelt reelected

—Rodgers and Hammerstein, *Oklahoma*

1945—Germany crushed—surrenders—Hitler commits suicide

—Mussolini killed in Italy by Italians

—V-E Day

—Yalta Conference

—Roosevelt dies

—Truman becomes thirty-third president

—Atomic bombs dropped on Hiroshima and Nagasaki

—United Nations founded

—T. S. Eliot wins the Nobel Prize

—Eleanor Roosevelt appointed delegate to the United Nations

—Ezra Pound charged with treason

BIBLIOGRAPHY

Cather, Willa. *My Antonia.* Thorndike Press, Thorndike, Maine: 1986.

Cooke, Alistair. *Alistair Cooke's America.* New York: Knopf, 1974.

Doctorow, E. L. *Ragtime.* New York: Fawcett, 1987.

Chief, D. Eagle, *Winter Count.* Denver, CO: Golden Bell Press, 1968.

Eliot, T. S. *Old Possum's Book of Practical Cats.* San Diego, CA: Harcourt Brace Jovanovich, 1982.

Fitzgerald, F. Scott. *The Great Gatsby.* New York: Scribner's, 1983.

Givner, Joan. *Katharine Anne Porter: A Life.* New York: Simon and Schuster, 1982.

Heilman, Grant, ed. *Farm Town: A Memoir of the 1930s.* Lexington, NH: Greene, 1987.

Hemingway, Ernest. *For Whom the Bell Tolls.* New York: Scribner's, 1982.

Hersey, John. *Hiroshima.* New York: Random House, 1989.

Hynes, Samuel. *Flights of Passage: Reflections of a World War II Aviator.* Annapolis, MD: Naval Institute Press, 1988.

Lash, Joseph P. *Eleanor and Franklin.* New York: Norton, 1971.

McCullers, Carson. *The Heart Is a Lonely Hunter.* New York: Bantam, 1983.

———. *Member of the Wedding.* New York: Bantam, 1985.

Mitford, Nancy. *Zelda: A Biography.* New York: Harper and Row, 1970.

Rudnick, Lois Palken. *Mabel Dodge Lujan: New Woman, New Worlds.* Albuquerque: University of New Mexico Press, 1984.

Standing Bear, Luther. *My People, the Sioux.* Boston: Houghton Mifflin, 1928.

Steinbeck, John. *The Grapes of Wrath.* New York: Penguin, 1977.

Thurber, James. *My World—and Welcome to It.* San Diego, CA: Harcourt Brace Jovanovich, 1969.

Weems, John Edward. *Peary: The Explorer and the Man.* Los Angeles: Tarcher, 1987.

Welty, Eudora. *The Optimist's Daughter.* New York: Random House, 1972.

Wright, Richard. *Black Boy.* New Directions, 1969.

Wouk, Herman. *War and Remembrance.* Boston: Little, Brown, 1978.

———. *Winds of War.* Boston: Little, Brown, 1971.

Name ______________________________ Date ______________

6-1. THE FRONTIER

Although technically no longer in existence, the frontier was still celebrated in the literature of the twentieth century. The frontier always represented certain characteristics. Below, match the qualities listed with a frontier-type character found in the literature of the period. Use at least three different stories as source material.

CHARACTERISTIC	CHARACTER	AUTHOR
Self-reliance		
Courage		
Pride		
Honesty		
Strength		
Freedom		

Name three different ways in which characteristics of the frontier survive today in the United States.

1. ______________________________

____

____

2. ______________________________

____

____

3. ______________________________

____

____

Name ______________________________ Date ______________

6-2. THE DREAM CRASHES

You are part of the 1920s Jazz Age, perhaps very much like some of F. Scott Fitzgerald's characters. Below, describe your life, including attitudes, expectations, and values before and after the crash of 1929, which ushered in the Great Depression.

CRASH

	JAZZ AGE	GREAT DEPRESSION
Job		
Lifestyle		
In the news		
Values		
Expectations		

Which column above best describes Americans of today? Explain.

____

____

____

____

____

____

Name ______________________________ Date ______________

6-3. DOWN ON THE FARM

Many authors were showing a movement from the farm or frontier to the city. The character making the physical change also made an internal change. These changes brought about a new understanding and mental, spiritual, or emotional growth.

DIRECTIONS: Choose an author who portrayed a character moving from a rural area to the city and fill in the information below.

Title ______________________________ Author ______________

Name of character ______________________________

1. What was lost or left behind?

____

____

____

2. What trials and hardships occurred?

____

____

____

____

____

3. What was gained?

____

____

____

4. What characteristics stayed with this person through it all?

____

____

____

____

Name ______________________________ Date ______________

6-4. THE SOUTH RISES

During this time the South produced a great body of literature, universal in nature, though regional in setting. To get a general picture of this literature, fill in the chart. Choose the material of different authors from which to gather your information.

Authors
1.
2.
3.
4.

SOUTHERN LITERATURE

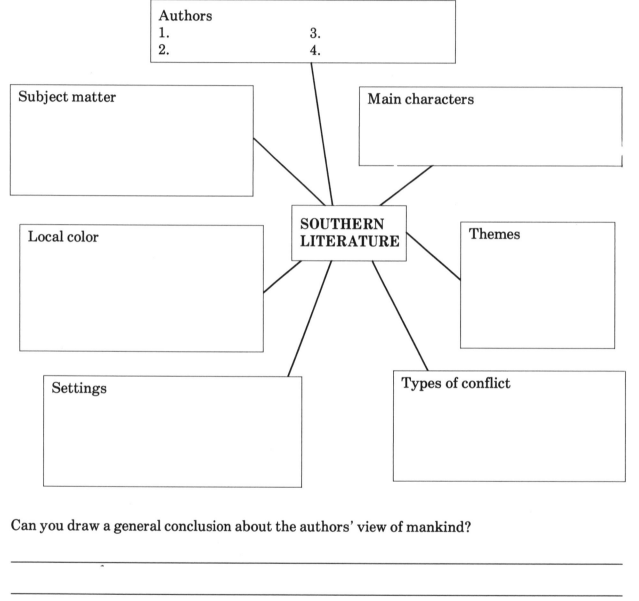

Subject matter

Main characters

Local color

Themes

Settings

Types of conflict

Can you draw a general conclusion about the authors' view of mankind?

____

____

____

____

____

Name ______________________ Date ______________

6-5. WOMEN IN LITERATURE

Let us take a look at the women in the literature of this age to see if attitudes toward them and attitudes held by them are changing in this century. First, look at one woman in a work by a male author and answer the questions below. Then look at one in a work by a female author and answer those same three questions. You may write the answers in a paragraph format rather than the question-and-answer format if you choose.

1. What is she like?
2. What does she do?
3. What does she think about?

Male author ______________________

Title ______________________

Character 1 ______________________

____

____

____

____

____

____

____

Female author ______________________

Title ______________________

Character 2 ______________________

____

____

____

____

____

____

____

Name ______________________________ Date ______________

6-6. I OBJECT

Social protest has been part of American literature from its beginning. One of our strengths as a society has been the right to disagree with the way things are.

DIRECTIONS: Trace social protest through American history. Find two examples of this type of literature from two previous ages and two from the era being studied. Then, fill in the information below.

PREVIOUS AGES

Example 1:

Title and author ______________________________

What was being protested? ______________________________

____

____

Example 2:

Title and author ______________________________

What was being protested? ______________________________

____

____

FROM THE TWENTIETH CENTURY

Example 1:

Title and author ______________________________

What was being protested? ______________________________

____

____

Example 2:

Title and author ______________________________

What was being protested? ______________________________

____

____

Name ______________________________ Date ______________

6-7. "THE TRUE ESSENCE OF CIVILIZATION"

Native Americans were also contemplating their universe and values. Chief Luther Standing Bear wrote the following:

> The man who sat on the ground in his tipi meditating on life and its meaning, accepting the kinship of all creatures and acknowledging unity with the universe of things was infusing into his being the true essence of civilization. And when native man left off this form of development, his humanization was retarded in growth.

What is Chief Standing Bear saying? Put his ideas into your own words.

____

____

____

____

____

____

____

____

What would you say is Chief Standing Bear's definition of *civilization*?

____

____

____

____

Name another author from this era who would agree with Luther Standing Bear. Why?

____

____

____

____

Name ______________________________ Date ______________

6-8. ABOUT TOWN TONIGHT

A famous poet, Carl Sandburg or Robert Frost maybe, is coming to town to read his poetry. This is an event that draws large crowds. You are an Arts and Leisure reporter and your editor has assigned you to write an article on the artist and on the upcoming event to interest and inform your readers. Write your story below. You may want to read one or two such articles from your newspaper before you do your own to make certain of the form you will use and the type of information you will include.

Headline ______________________________

Byline ______________________________

Name ______________________________ Date ____________

6-9. ALIENATION

Loneliness, isolation, and alienation became prominent themes in American literature during this time. This emptiness was often caused by shattered dreams and ideals.

DIRECTIONS: Choose two main characters in either prose or poetry who felt a sense of loneliness, alienation, or spiritual emptiness and determine: (1) How exactly the character felt, (2) what caused the feeling, and (3) whether the feeling eventually went away and why or why not. Fill in all of the information below.

Main character 1 ______________________________

Title and author ______________________________

Main character 2 ______________________________

Title and author ______________________________

	Character 1	Character 2
1.		
2.		
3.		

Name *five* things that happened during this time that caused these feelings in people.

____

____

____

____

____

Name ______________________________ Date ______________

6-10. AMERICAN HUMOR

Mark Twain and James Thurber were both humorists. In fact, it has been said that Thurber is Twain's literary descendant. Compare the two authors by filling in the information below.

DESCRIPTION OF A MAIN CHARACTER

TWAIN	THURBER
Name of character	
Author's feelings toward the character	
A humorous situation	
Theme of story	
Examples of diction	

1. Judging from this information, how are the two writers alike?

2. How are they different?

Name ______________________________ Date ______________

6-11. "THE WOODS ARE LOVELY . . ."

The talent to describe a scene with meaning and immediacy in a few words was demonstrated again and again by twentieth-century poets. Try it. Choose a scene described in a poem in your book, a type of scene with which you are familiar. It could be snow falling in a forest or a foggy city street. Below, write your description of the scene. Include any personal feelings the scene arouses in you.

Scene ______________________________

Description ______________________________

Now, on the back of this sheet, copy the same sort of scene from this poem or another in your text. Notice the amount of meaning packed into a few lines by the careful choice of words and use of figurative language. On the back of this page or on another paper, rewrite your description, keeping the same scene but using fewer words.

Name ______________________________ Date ______________

6-12. GOOD GRIEF! NOW WHERE?!

Significant changes in *plot* appear in the first half of the twentieth century. Chronology often took second place to associations and remembrances in the mind of characters. So it often takes mental gymnastics while reading these stories to keep events in order. The challenge, however, is well worth the effort; some of this literature is truly great.

DIRECTIONS: Choose a story from this period, perhaps one by Faulkner in which the plot does not proceed in chronological order, and put events in order.

Title and author: ______________________________

Incident 1 (in time) ______________________________

____

____

Incident 2 ______________________________

____

____

Incident 3 ______________________________

____

____

Incident 4 ______________________________

____

____

Incident 5 ______________________________

____

____

Incident 7 ______________________________

____

____

Incident 8 ______________________________

____

Name ______________________________ Date ______________

6-13. IT'S NOT WHAT YOU SAY . . .

Style is the manner in which an author talks to us through his or her writing. We can make generalizations about the style of writing of a particular author by noticing certain characteristics of the writing.

DIRECTIONS: Compare the styles of writing of Hemingway and Faulkner by analyzing four characteristics. Read the stories, choose representative examples of the listed characteristics, then draw a conclusion about each. On another piece of paper, write a basic five-paragraph expository composition comparing the way in which these two authors do their work.

HEMINGWAY	FAULKNER
Word choice Examples Conclusion	
Sentence length Examples Conclusion	
Sentence variety (types) Examples Conclusion	
Figures of speech and imagery Examples Conclusion	

Name ______________________________ Date ______________

6-14. THAT REMINDS ME

Twentieth-century authors, inspired in part by Freud, attempted to look inside their characters and to record what was there—exactly what was there. A modern technique called *stream of consciousness* provided the means for this. Stream of consciousness is a style of writing that attempts to reproduce the flow of a character's thoughts, feelings, associations, mental images, and memories as they occur, with no regard to order, logic, or grammatical correctness. James Joyce perfected this revolutionary technique, and many American authors used a form of it, among them Faulkner, Porter, and Eliot.

DIRECTIONS: Choose a passage that you feel is written in the stream-of-consciousness technique and copy it below. Then, on the back of this paper, make a list of the different trains of thought that ran through the character's head.

Title ______________________________ Author ______________________

____

____

____

____

____

____

____

____

____

____

____

____

____

____

____

____

____

Name ______________________________ Date ______________

6-15. MY HERO!

A new type of protagonist, the *anti-hero,* made an appearance in the literature of this era. The character is not heroic and does not stand out in a crowd. He or she is just an ordinary person trying to make it through life. The anti-hero is sometimes overwhelmed by it all but struggles on, trying to understand and to cope with life.

DIRECTIONS: Choose a protagonist from the literature of this period who is an anti-hero. Describe the character and his or her life. Include two of his or her major struggles. Then do the same for a main character from another story who is a more typical protagonist.

ANTI-HERO

Title and author ______________________________

Description ______________________________

____

____

____

____

HERO

Title and author ______________________________

Description ______________________________

____

____

____

____

Which of the two characters comes closer to being like you? Why?

Name ______________________________ Date ______________

6-16. SPEAK TO ME IN IAMBIC

Blank verse is poetry written in unrhymed iambic pentameter. It has been determined that this form closely approximates ordinary English. In other words, we often talk in iambs. If you scan the previous line, you will see this. Since blank verse usually sounds natural, it appears to be an easy form to use; however, it requires talent to write well in blank verse. This form also lends itself to the expression of grand passions; Shakespeare, Marlowe, Milton, Wordsworth, Coleridge, and Tennyson, as well as many twentieth-century poets, wrote in blank verse.

DIRECTIONS: Choose ten lines of poetry that appear to be written in blank verse. Copy the lines below and scan them to see if you were correct. At the bottom of the page note any variations in meter.

Title and author ______________________________

____

____

____

____

____

____

____

____

____

Variations ______________________________

____

____

____

DIRECTIONS: Choose one variation in rhythm and tell what it added to the meaning of the poem.

Name ______________________________ Date ______________

6-17. THE PRAIRIE SLUMBERS

Personification is a figure of speech in which an author gives human qualities to inanimate objects, animals, or abstract concepts. It is an excellent device for conveying pictures and ideas with few words. For example, in one of his poems Carl Sandburg has the moon "walking," "peering," and "seeing."

DIRECTIONS: Find three examples of personification in the poetry of the era and fill in the information below.

ANIMAL OR OBJECT	HUMAN QUALITY	TITLE AND AUTHOR
1.		
2.		
3.		

Another very effective figure of speech is the *apostrophe.* This occurs when someone or something not present is spoken to as though it were present and could answer, i.e., "Jefferson, where are you when we need you?"

DIRECTIONS: Find two examples of apostrophe in the poetry of the era and fill in the information below.

EXAMPLE	PERSON OR OBJECT ADDRESSED	TITLE AND AUTHOR
1.		
2.		

DIRECTIONS: Try your hand. Write one original example of personification and one of apostrophe.

Personification ______________________________

____

Apostrophe ______________________________

____

Name ______________________________ Date ______________

6-18. FOLLOW THE IMAGE

Imagism was an early twentieth-century poetic movement led by Ezra Pound. The imagists were in revolt against poetic conventions of the time. Their chief concern was to present a hard, clear *image* and to use very exact words to do so. The imagists believed in absolute freedom in the choice of subject, the use of common speech, and the creation of new rhythms. Poets who wrote in this style included H. D., Amy Lowell, William Carlos Williams, and Carl Sandburg.

DIRECTIONS: Choose one poem written in the imagist style and follow the image through the poem. Do this by first noticing each word that the poet uses that relates to the basic image. Then write the description of the image in your own words but include in your description the list of words you pulled from the poem. Underline these words in your description. Use the back of this paper if necessary.

Title and author ______________________________

Object or person described ______________________________

List of words related to basic description ______________________________

____

____

Description in your own words with poet's words underlined ______________________________

____

____

____

____

____

____

____

____

____

____

____

____

____

6-19. VOCABULARY LIST

1. abject
2. abrogate
3. abrupt
4. accolade
5. anachronism
6. andiron
7. anemia
8. apotheosis
9. arrogant
10. austere
11. bisect
12. blatant
13. coalesce
14. constrict
15. desolate
16. dirge
17. dissolution
18. droned
19. dyspepsia
20. ecru
21. effluvium
22. elemental
23. enormity
24. epitome
25. excruciating
26. exemplary
27. fallible
28. fallow
29. fatuous
30. foray
31. fortuitous
32. furtive
33. gambit
34. gaunt
35. humility
36. indomitable
37. insidious
38. interminable
39. iridescent
40. jocularity
41. judicious
42. kinetic
43. limber
44. luminous
45. malevolent
46. malinger
47. medley
48. mottle
49. mundane
50. myriad
51. nebulous
52. nimbus
53. obliterate
54. opalescent
55. opiate
56. pedantic
57. petulance
58. plaintive
59. pompous
60. priggish
61. progenitor
62. prolonged
63. pugilist
64. rakish
65. rancor
66. sadistic
67. scourge
68. somnolent
69. suffice
70. surfeit
71. temerity
72. unseemly
73. veranda
74. vigorously
75. wanton

Name ______________________________ Date ______________

6-20. FIT FOR THE OCCASION

Formal English, as the phrase implies, is used for formal written and spoken occasions. It is used in making most speeches, in textbooks or any serious writing, job interviews, and any occasion that is serious or dignified. It is usually used in conjunction with a careful choice of words and a more complex sentence structure.

DIRECTIONS: Write two sentences that could be characterized as formal English. In each use three words from the vocabulary list.

1. ______________________________

____

____

____

2. ______________________________

____

____

____

Informal English is used for occasions that are casual and more everyday in nature. The words are used regularly in ordinary conversation, and the sentence structure is usually simple. We use informal English for most social occasions, in writing or speaking of those occasions, and in daily conversation.

DIRECTIONS: Write two sentences that could be characterized as informal English. In each use two words from the vocabulary list.

1. ______________________________

____

____

2. ______________________________

____

____

Substandard English is characterized by a lack of correct grammar and sentence structure and a very limited vocabulary. Its use, of course, is discouraged. *Nonstandard English* refers to various ethnic or geographic dialects whose grammars and vocabularies vary from standard English. It should not be used in formal situations.

Name ______________________ Date ____________

6-21. CROSSWORD

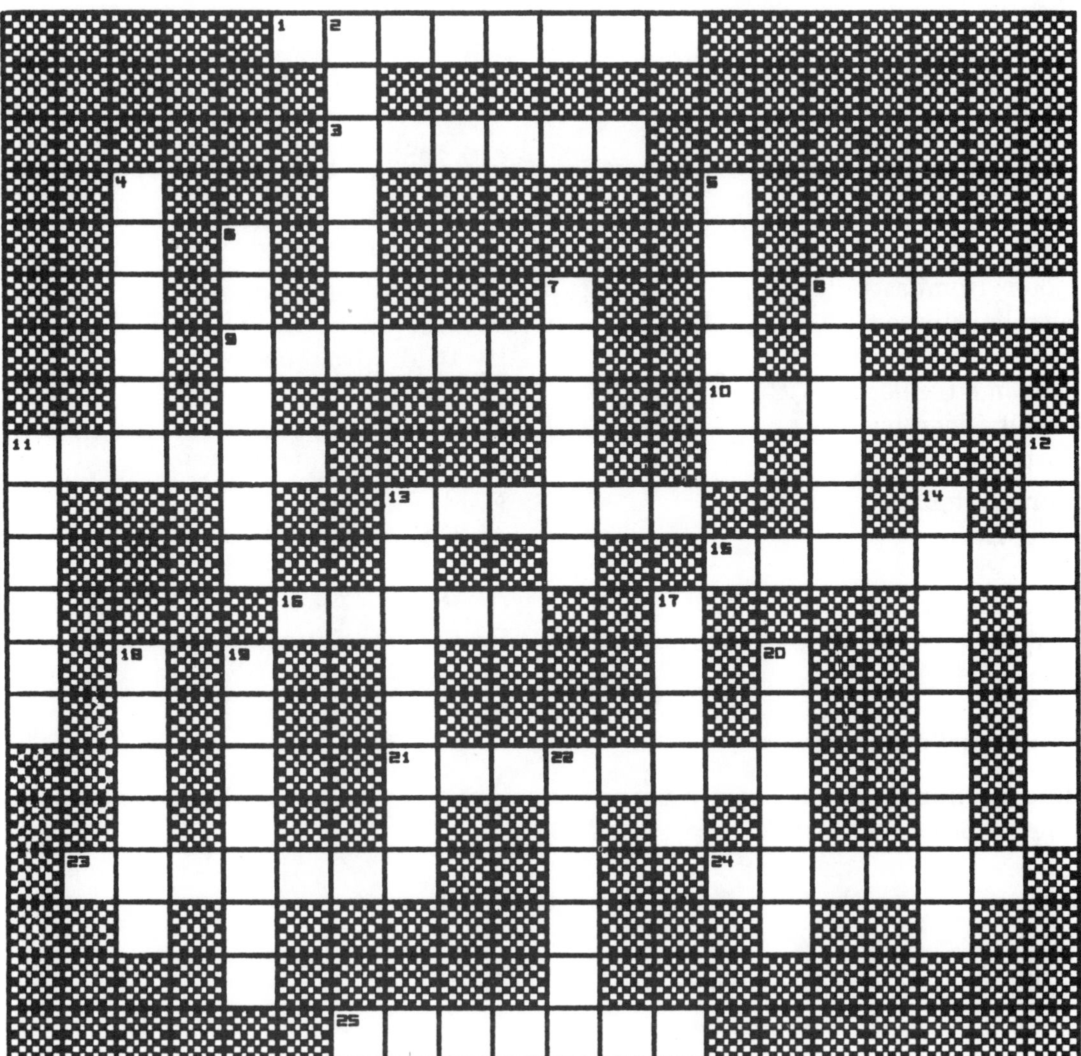

ACROSS
1. deliberately cruel
3. made a low humming sound
8. thin and bony
9. ordinary
10. pliable, flexible
11. bitter resentment
13. contemptible, wretched
15. inane, stupid
16. funeral hymn
21. approval, praise
23. stealthy, shifty
24. to divide into two
25. oversupply

DOWN
2. fireplace fixture
4. immoral, lewd, cruel
5. cover with spots
6. pretentious, overly dignified
7. assortment, mixture
8. opening move
11. showy, jaunty appearance
12. not in good taste
13. annul
14. squeeze, contract
17. initial attempt or raid
18. halo, aura
19. related to motion
20. blood deficiency
22. sedative narcotic

Name ______________________________ Date ______________

6-22. THINK IT THROUGH

Analogies

1. Fallible : Infallible ::
   A. Mundane : Ordinary
   B. Arrogant : Humble
   C. Temerity : Audacity
   D. Surfeit : Suffice
   E. Rakish : Brackish
2. Pompous : Bombastic ::
   A. Seemly : Unseemly
   B. Ecru: Red
   C. Prolonged : Short
   D. Fallow : Inactive
   E. Furtive : Restive
3. Andiron : Fireplace ::
   A. Loft : Barn
   B. Iron : Press
   C. City : Street
   D. Bum : Hobo
   E. Fire : Heat
4. Temerity : Enormity ::
   A. Petulance : Petulant
   B. Gaunt : Flaunt
   C. Kinetic : Science
   D. Humility : Jollity
   E. Rancor : Hatred
5. Pugilist : Ring ::
   A. Hoopster : Basket
   B. Bride : Bouquet
   C. Diva : Stage
   D. Shortstop : Glove
   E. Umpire : Referee
6. Field : Fallow ::
   A. City : Village
   B. Farm : Plow
   C. Forest : Trees
   D. School : Education
   E. Jungle : Lush

Synonyms and Antonyms

You will find a synonym and an antonym answer for each word below. Mark the synonyms with an S and the antonyms with an A.

1. Gaunt
   A. Hungry B. Fearful C. Thin D. Inept E. Obese
2. Fatuous
   A. Overweight B. Sensible C. Bony D. Stupid E. Lovable
3. Insidious
   A. Treacherous B. Judicious C. Aboveboard D. Rakish E. Plaintive
4. Iridescent
   A. Indecent B. Gray C. Falling D. Sunlight E. Colorful
5. Somnolent
   A. Unattractive B. Alert C. Lost D. Walking E. Drowsy

Section 7
INTO THE FUTURE

1946 - Williams to Angelou

SKILLS INDEX

Skill	Worksheet	
	7-13	New Words for New Things
	7-3	The Sixties
Comparison and contrast	7-8	Hang On
	7-2	Old vs. New
Deductive reasoning	7-8	Hang On
	7-14	Into the Future
	7-19	The Part Is the Whole
Drawing Conclusions	7-9	All for One, One for All
	7-7	Growing Up
	7-14	Into the Future
	7-16	Real or Imagined?
Generalizing	7-8	Hang On
Inductive reasoning	7-3	The Sixties
Synthesizing	7-9	All for One, One for All
	7-7	Growing Up
	7-6	Lead On
	7-13	New Words for New Things

Vocabulary Skills	**Worksheet**	
Analogies, synonyms, antonyms	7-22	Think It Through
Statement of fact and opinion	7-21	You Don't Say
Generalizing	7-21	You Don't Say
Cause/effect, Either/or	7-21	You Don't Say

Other Skills	**Worksheet**	
Role playing	7-10	Today
Stage setting	7-12	On Stage

WORKSHEET NOTES

7-1. History and Literature

7-2. Old vs. New

The first exercise reminds students that literature today, as in the past, reflects the society from which it arises. The four topics listed in the worksheet are basic to the era, and students should not have trouble finding literature dealing with them. The second worksheet connects today's literature with that of such authors as Melville, Poe, and Hawthorne, while reviewing basic literary themes. Links to the idealism vs. realism conflicts of authors like Tennessee Williams will become fairly obvious as students get into the work.

7-3. The Sixties

The 1960s set the stage for revolution from within. Many students can do this exercise fairly quickly if they let one thought immediately lead to others; names, dates, and events will come to mind. For example, civil rights may bring to mind boycotts, sit-ins, marches, riots, Watts, Martin Luther King, Jr., voter registration, fire hoses, Malcolm X, and Medgar Evers. The counterculture will remind students of love-ins, drop out, turn on, "Make love not war," "cool," Berkeley, Haight-Ashbury, and granny glasses and love beads. Heroes could be J. F. Kennedy (Cuba, missile crisis, Dallas, Peace Corps), Martin Luther King, Jr. (Freedom March, "I Have a Dream," Montgomery-Selma March), Cesar Chavez. Feminists such as Gloria Steinem could also come to mind. The era was a time of movements: feminist, farmers (tractors in D.C.), native American protests (Mt. Rushmore) are three examples.

7-4. Dear Editor

This is the seventh worksheet that asks students to be aware of the types of writing found in newspapers. The previous exercise presented ideas, although local issues are plentiful. Perhaps it could be suggested that students write a rough draft on another sheet of paper before committing the final copy to the worksheet. After all, readers will judge the author of the letter while considering the points presented. One or two of the letters could be sent to the local newspaper.

7-5. From Life

Once again, this exercise asks students to note the idea that literature comes from life, that authors write about what they know, or, at the very least, that this serves as a starting point. This is one of the ways in which authors write convincingly and give their works verity. It may be a good idea to have the students do this exercise for two or three authors like Albee, Williams, and Hansberry, so that they can see the consistency of this idea.

7-6. Lead On

Sometimes we cannot see our heroes when they are among us; they seem so human. From the past, names such as Washington, Jefferson, Lincoln, Dolly Madison, Nathan

Hale, Grant, Lee, Daniel Boone, Earhart, Lindbergh, and others appear readily. Names from today will be more difficult for students to come by. The areas of space (John Glenn, Neil Armstrong), medicine (Jonas Salk), and the military (Schwarzkopf), among others, will yield some names. It will be interesting to see if the old frontier qualities of independence, courage, and self-reliance still play the major part in the students' descriptions or whether such qualities as optimism, selflessness, self-knowledge, and gentleness will also be part of the picture.

7-7. Growing Up

7-8. Hang On

These two exercises ask students to do some fairly sophisticated thinking regarding societal and personal values and to apply them to their country and to their own lives. The conclusions drawn will certainly give a chance to assess those values that are a permanent part of a mature person's and a mature country's lives. What becomes important—family and home; honesty; faith and religion, spirituality; freedom; education; possessions; financial freedom and power—tells us much about the society in which we live. Of course, some of the authors who depict loneliness, confusion, injustice, materialism, or a striving to understand life do not find a solution. Students may notice this also. The suggestions listed above are generic in nature. When the students choose their authors, more specific problems and ways of handling them will be apparent.

7-9. All for One, One for All

This era, especially, has authors writing about the group of people from which they came, fairly recent immigrant groups as well as native Americans, hispanics, and African Americans. All are represented in literature by their own spokespersons. Even though people differ in terms of customs, beliefs, clothing, food, music, and physical features, everyone has certain basic goals and values. All honor such things as family, freedom, education, honesty, and courage. All want success and happiness, and security. All must find ways of existing happily in the world as it is. Preferably, students will draw the conclusion that people are more alike than different.

7-10. Today

This seemingly simple exercise asks students to be aware of style, society, and characterization as they write. It might be fun for the teacher to read these to the class and have the students guess the character.

7-11. Turn About

Since much of what students write is in the essay form, this exercise reviews some basic composition terms and ideas. It allows students to do some literary analysis in the process. Students may need to be reminded of such style characteristics as word choice, sentence length and type, and formal and informal English.

7-12. On Stage

This should be fun for students. They will need to read or reread only the introductions, stage directions, and part of one act to do the worksheet. While they do this, they must visualize the stage, then draw it as best they can. Terms such as *stage left* and *stage right* could be introduced here.

7-13. New Words for New Things

This worksheet will provide students with an enjoyable way to reflect on language and change. When finished, students could put their answers on the board or on butcher paper to see how many new words they have. They could also put a check by the old words with new meanings. For the category of choice, students might choose education or recreation. Sample answers for the five categories follow: travel = jet (Concorde), space shuttle, motel, turbocharged, Samsonite; business = fax, modem, input, word processor, robot, call forwarding; war/defense = nuclear submarine, nuclear bomb, stealth bomber, Star Wars, SAM (surface-to-air missile); science/medicine = clone, skylab, laser, transplant, biofeedback, CAT scan, MRI; new products = computer, microwave, video cassette recorder, compact disc.

7-14. Into the Future

The last worksheet in this section asks students to use their knowledge of characterization as they visualize the future. The teacher can suggest that students use themselves instead of a fictional character if they wish. Their views of the future could be very enlightening, or scary.

7-15. Fish or Fowl?

7-16. Real or Imagined?

7-17. See and Tell

7-18. It All Depends

7-19. The Part is the Whole

This part of Section 7 introduces or reviews some fundamental literary terms. "Fish or Fowl" introduces the idea of *genre* and reviews basic types of literature. Students should find this easy. The teacher may limit the poetry in this worksheet or instruct students to stop when the categories are full. "Real or Imagined" can be used as a book report form for outside or extra reading. "See and Tell" reviews basic literary terms associated with analyzing fiction. It could be helpful to have students write on the back of the paper their opinions of the show as a literary work. "It All Depends" reviews the concept of point of view and asks students to do some fairly mature analysis in connection with it. The class might also be reminded that the basic point of the exercise holds true in real life. To point this out, students could do the exercise about an actual incident from two perspectives. *Metonymy* and *synecdoche* are introduced in the last of these worksheets. Examples that might be used are blue and gray for Union and Confederate forces, hardhat for a construction worker, the bench for a judge. "The pen is mightier than the sword" contains two examples. Referring to a strong person as "a back" is another.

7-20. Vocabulary List

7-21. You Don't Say

7-22. Think It Through

The vocabulary section consists of three worksheets. The first and last are familiar; "You Don't Say" reviews common composition terms. Example sentences for each follow in order: Beautiful *mosaics* were found in the ruins of Pompeii. No *ribald* statements should appear in generally available reading material. All politicians are *glib.* Poor *mastication* can result in indigestion. You must either *meditate* regularly or you will remain tense. Answers for "Thinking It Through" follow:

Answers

	Analogies	Synonyms	Antonyms
1.	C (antonyms)	A	B
2.	A (synonyms)	C	A
3.	E (action and object of)	B	D
4.	E (description of)	C	B
5.	B (whole to part)	B	E
6.	B (synonyms)		

PROJECT IDEAS

Today's Authors

Make a display of references to authors and literature of today in current media. The whole class can watch for items in newspapers and magazines. Include copies of current bestseller lists. Also include a U.S. map marked with places today's authors live or were born.

Take a Poll

Take a "Person-in-the-Hall" Poll. Ask questions like the following:

Whom do you most admire?
What quality in people do you most admire?
What characteristic do you need most to succeed in life?
What is the most important problem we face now?
What is the best thing happening right now?

Add questions of your own. Use the results of the poll to make a chart or graph for classroom display. Does it reflect the ideas found in the literature of this era?

My Town, Then and Now

Take two sets of photos of your town. The first set would make it seem like a town of a hundred years ago; the second set would show your town to be thoroughly modern. Set up a portable classroom display to illustrate how the past and present coexist.

Poets and Music

Choose music that fits the mood and theme of four of the poems in the text. Display the poems and play the music for the class.

Research

Research the following for written or oral presentations: Elvis, modern musicals, unmanned space exploration, war in the Persian Gulf, baby boomers, Kennedy's inaugural speech, the Peace Corps, the Equal Rights Amendment, American Book Award, the personal computer revolution, the hydrogen bomb, the environment, Watts, the feminist movement, Senator Joseph McCarthy, Rosa Parks, an eminent stage actor or actress, the *Challenger,* Sandra Day O'Connor, Martin Luther King, Jr., the Beat Generation, Wounded Knee II, Thurgood Marshall, *Brown* vs. *The Board of Education*, Vietnam, Watergate, polio, man on the moon, or any other topic from the chronology.

Design a Car

Draw a picture of the "car" as it may look twenty years from now. What kind of engine will it have? Do a magazine ad.

CHRONOLOGY

1946—O'Neill, *The Iceman Cometh*
—United Nation's first meeting, London
—Winston Churchill's Iron Curtain speech, Missouri
1947—Williams, *A Streetcar Named Desire*
—First annual Tony Awards
1949—Faulkner wins Nobel Prize
—Miller, *Death of a Salesman*
1950-1954—Korean War
1952—Ellison, *The Invisible Man*
—Steinbeck, *East of Eden*
—Eisenhower elected president
1953—Miller, *The Crucible*
—McCarthy hearings, Washington, D.C.
—Rosenbergs executed
—Polio vaccine, Dr. Jonas Salk
1954—*Brown* vs. *Board of Education of Topeka*
—Hemingway wins Nobel Prize
—Air Force Academy established
1955—Rosa Parks refuses to move to the back of the bus
—Williams, *Cat on a Hot Tin Roof*
1956—O'Neill, *Long Day's Journey into Night*
1958—TV's quiz program scandals
1959—Hansberry, *A Raisin in the Sun*, produced
1960—Sit-ins begin, North Carolina
—John Fitzgerald Kennedy elected president
1961—Steinbeck, *The Winter of Our Discontent*
—Peace Corps established
—Berlin Wall erected
—U.S. commitment in Vietnam expands
1962—Lincoln Center opens, New York City
—Cuban missile crisis

—Steinbeck wins Nobel Prize

1963—Freedom March, Washington, D.C.

—Guthrie Theater opens, Minneapolis

—President Kennedy assassinated, Dallas

1964—Johnson elected president

—Racial demonstrations and urban violence escalate

1966—National Organization for Women founded

1967—First heart transplant, South Africa

1968—Steinbeck dies

—Martin Luther King and Robert Kennedy assassinated

—Nixon elected president

1969—Neil Armstrong walks on the moon; live TV broadcast

1971—Kennedy Center opens, Washington, D.C.

1972—Welty, *The Optimist's Daughter*

—Watergate break-in

—President Nixon visits China; Nixon reelected

—O'Connor, *The Complete Stories*

1973—Vietnam cease-fire

1974—Nixon resigns under threat of impeachment; Ford becomes president

1976—Bellow wins Nobel Prize

—Carter elected president

—National bicentennial celebration

—U.S. Viking I lands on Mars and conducts soil tests

1978—Singer wins Nobel Prize

—Jefferson Davis regains U.S. citizenship posthumously

1979—Iranians seize U.S. embassy in Teheran; ninety hostages held

1980—Reagan elected president

1983—Tennessee Williams dies

1985—Space shuttle *Challenger* explodes, killing six astronauts and one schoolteacher

1986—Nation celebrates the Statue of Liberty's centennial

—Nuclear power plant accident at Chernobyl

1987—Stock market crash

1988—Bush elected president

1989—The Berlin Wall comes down

—Spacecraft *Atlantis* begins its six-year voyage to Jupiter

—United States invades Panama; Noriega brought to Miami

—*Exxon Valdez* runs aground, spills oil in Prince William Sound

1990—Iraq overruns and annexes Kuwait; United States and others send military forces

—President Mikhail Gorbachev wins the Nobel Peace Prize

—Octavio Paz of Mexico wins the Nobel Prize for Literature

1991—War in the Persian Gulf

—Steinbeck, *Grapes of Wrath* becomes a stage hit

—Best picture, *Dances with Wolves*

BIBLIOGRAPHY

Angelou, Maya. *I Know Why the Caged Bird Sings.* New York: Random House, 1970.

Asimov, Isaac. *The Foundation Trilogy.* New York: Octopus/Heinemann, 1981.

Berry, Thomas. *The Dream of the Earth.* San Francisco: Sierra Club Books, 1988.

Bishop, Jim. *The Day Kennedy Was Shot.* New York: Funk and Wagnalls, 1968.

Bradbury, Ray. *Fahrenheit 451.* New York: Ballantine, 1976.

Branch, Taylor. *Parting the Waters, 1954-1963.* New York: Simon and Schuster, 1988.

Cheever, John. *The Wapshot Chronicle.* New York: Harper and Row, 1989.

Clarke, Arthur C. *The Songs of Distant Earth.* New York: Ballantine, 1986.

Gassner, John. *A Treasury of the Theatre.* New York: Simon and Schuster, 1968.

Hawkins, Stephen W. *A Brief History of Time.* New York: Bantam, 1988.

Hersey, John. *Hiroshima.* New York: Random House, 1989.

Keillor, Garrison. *We Are Still Married.* New York: Viking, 1989.

Lincoln, Kenneth. *The Good Red Road.* New York: Harper and Row, 1987.

Lopez, Barry. *Arctic Dreams.* New York: Bantam, 1986.

Momaday, N. Scott. *House Made of Dawn.* New York: Harper and Row, 1976.

Morrison, Toni. *Beloved.* New York: Signet, 1991.

Plath, Sylvia. *The Bell Jar.* New York: Bantam, 1975.

Tan, Amy. *The Joy Luck Club.* New York: Ballantine, 1989.

Vonnegut, Kurt, Jr. *Breakfast of Champions.* New York: Dell, 1974.

Walker, Alice. *The Color Purple.* New York: Pocket Books, 1982.

———. *The Temple of My Familiar.* New York: Pocket Books, 1990.

Wiesel, Elie. *Twilight.* New York: Summit, 1987.

Wolfe, Tom. *The Bonfire of the Vanities.* New York: Bantam, 1990.

Name ______________________ Date ______________

7-1. HISTORY AND LITERATURE

More than at any time in its history, the United States has had to make major changes in society during this period. Sometimes this has been done quietly; sometimes attention has been drawn to problems in an aggressive manner. As was noted in other periods, major authors have reflected those changes in their works.

DIRECTIONS: Choose one author for each item listed and tell briefly that author's attitude about the subject.

1. War

   Author ______________________

   Attitude ______________________

   ____

2. Civil rights and the problems of minorities

   Author ______________________

   Attitude ______________________

   ____

3. The family

   Author ______________________

   Attitude ______________________

   ____

4. Concerns of women

   Author ______________________

   Attitude

   ____

What does reading good literature dealing with these subjects add to your understanding?

Name ______________________________ Date ______________

7-2. OLD VS. NEW

From the beginning, American literature has dealt with the conflict of good vs. evil or flesh vs. spirit. In this exercise we will note what form these themes take today.

DIRECTIONS: Choose one work for each of two authors of this period and fill in the information below.

1. Author 1 ______________________________

   Title ______________________________

   Two conflicts present

   a. ______________ vs. ______________

   b. ______________ vs. ______________

2. Author 2 ______________________________

   Title ______________________________

   Two conflicts present

   a. ______________ vs. ______________

   b. ______________ vs. ______________

3. In what way are the conflicts you have listed a modern example of the old conflicts of good vs. evil or flesh vs. spirit?

   Conflict 1 ______________________________

   ____

   Conflict 2 ______________________________

   ____

   Conflict 3 ______________________________

   ____

   Conflict 4 ______________________________

   ____

Name ______________________________ Date ______________

7-3. THE SIXTIES

The events of the 1960s began changes in society that are with us today and that inspired authors and others. The times were filled with wonderful people and organizations, and moments of anger, riots, and cynicism as well. All who lived during the sixties were forever affected by the times. Anyone who does not know what happened during that time can never truly understand our society today.

DIRECTIONS: See what you know about the 1960s. Fill in the chart below with the names of people, events, or organizations connected with each topic, then further break down each category as indicated.

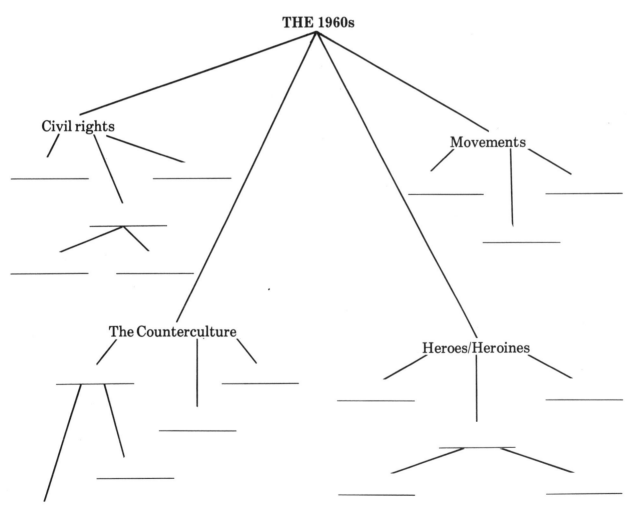

THE 1960s

Civil rights

Movements

The Counterculture

Heroes/Heroines

Name ______________________________ Date ______________

7-4. DEAR EDITOR

Our predecessors have always been willing to use the newspapers to air their views on any subject about which they had strong feelings. The editorial page has been a free forum to a large audience and has been instrumental not only in sharing personal views but also in calling attention to questionable practices by public officials.

DIRECTIONS: From the literature of this era choose a subject that concerns you. Put your ideas into a letter to the editor. Be specific and reasonable, and make certain that your spelling, punctuation, and grammar are correct. Remember the importance of a thesis statement and direct your letter to your audience.

Dear Editor:

____

____

____

____

____

____

____

____

____

____

____

____

____

____

____

____

____

Signature

____

Name ______________________________ Date ______________

7-5. FROM LIFE

Often, much of a good author's work appears to be autobiographical; elements of the works seem to come for the background of the author, for example, geography, dialect, family background, economic background, lifestyle, inner conflicts, and others.

DIRECTIONS: Choose an author and compare and contrast his or her life with one of his works. Do this by listing three items from the work that could have come from the author's life (A). Then list three items that appear not to have come from the author's life (B). You may use the categories listed above or you may choose your own. Make your answers very specific.

Author______________________________

Title______________________________

1. a. ______________________________

   ____

   b. ______________________________

   ____

2. a. ______________________________

   ____

   b. ______________________________

   ____

3. a. ______________________________

   ____

   b. ______________________________

   ____

If you were to write a play or short story, what elements from your life would find a place in the work? Explain why. Write your answer on the back of this paper.

Name ______________________ Date ____________

7-6. LEAD ON

It has been said that every age needs its heroes and heroines. Let us look at our heroes through the ages and determine what makes them worthy of admiration. Fill in the information below.

1. Name two people from life or from literature from each of two past eras whom you would consider heroic.

   a. Era 1 ______________________

   b. Heroes 1. ______________________

   2. ______________________

   c. In a few words and phrases, tell what characteristics made these people heroic.

   ____

   ____

   ____

   ____

   a. Era 2 ______________________

   b. Heroes 1. ______________________

   2. ______________________

   c. Characteristics ______________________

   ____

   ____

   ____

2. a. Today

   b. Heroes 1. ______________________

   2. ______________________

   c. Characteristics ______________________

   ____

   ____

   ____

Name ______________________________ Date ______________

7-7. GROWING UP

The United States is still fairly young, as nations go. It passed through a rugged adolescence into a troubled young adulthood. After over two hundred years as a nation, there are signs in the literature of the United States that it is truly growing up. A country matures in much the same way its citizens do.

DIRECTIONS: Below are listed some indicators of maturity. Choose a work of literature that deals with each. Then, in one or two sentences, show how the author depicted the quality.

1. Self-awareness
   Title and author ______________________________

   How depicted ______________________________

   ____

2. Long-term values
   Title and author ______________________________

   How depicted ______________________________

   ____

3. Acceptance of reality
   Title and author ______________________________

   How depicted ______________________________

   ____

4. Awareness of society's values
   Title and author ______________________________

   How depicted ______________________________

   ____

5. Honesty
   Title and author ______________________________

   How depicted ______________________________

   ____

Does your community as a whole shine in any of these areas?

____

Name ______________________________ Date ______________

7-8. HANG ON

Change occurs so quickly today that people often have difficulty finding a stable base for their lives. What does one cling to in an ever-changing world? Authors search for and often find answers that can enlighten us. A poet often tackles the subject directly; fiction authors can do so through their characters. Some, such as Faulkner, see a return to nature and a reconnection to the earth as a solution. Others find different answers.

DIRECTIONS: Choose three authors who have depicted this subject and fill in the information below.

1. Author and title(s) ______________________________

   Problem ______________________________

   Solution ______________________________

   ____

2. Author and title(s) ______________________________

   Problem ______________________________

   Solution ______________________________

   ____

3. Author and title(s) ______________________________

   Problem ______________________________

   Solution ______________________________

   ____

1. Are the solutions new and revolutionary or the age-old answers to such dilemmas?

   ____

   ____

2. Give two examples of authors from the past who have found the same solutions.

   ____

   ____

   ____

   ____

Name ______________________________ Date ______________

7-9. ALL FOR ONE, ONE FOR ALL

Several authors focus on specific groups of people; that is, much of the writing of this era is ethnic in nature. For example, Malamud and Singer depict Jewish life in their writings. However, even though the group has common traits, customs, and beliefs, the theme, messages, or ideas of the works are universal in nature; the lessons and insights go beyond the group.

DIRECTIONS: Choose an author whose writings focus on a specific group and fill in the information.

Author ______________________________

Title(s) ______________________________

Group of people ______________________________

List two *customs* that the people in this group have in common.

1. ______________________________
2. ______________________________

List two *beliefs* that the people in this group have in common.

1. ______________________________
2. ______________________________

List two other things that help make these people part of a specific group.

1. ______________________________
2. ______________________________

List two ways in which the members of this group are like people anywhere.

1. ______________________________
2. ______________________________

What universal idea or theme can we learn from this author's work?

____

____

____

____

Name ______________________________ Date ______________

7-10. TODAY

You are a person from the literature of the era. It is late, but before you go to sleep, you want to tell your journal about your day.

DIRECTIONS: Do a journal entry for the character you are. As you tell about the day—your successes, failures, concerns, joys, people in your life—use what you know about yourself. Use the correct style of writing, diction, and word choices. Stay within the same mood and have the same priorities as the character.

Character ______________________________

Title and author ______________________________

Date ______________ Location ______________________________

Journal entry ______________________________

Name ______________________ Date ____________

7-11. TURN ABOUT

You have written essays and had them analyzed and judged. Now it is your turn. Analyze an essay that you have read by filling in the information below. If you need more room, use the back of this page to continue your answers.

1. Title and author ______________________

2. What is the thesis? ______________________

3. What are the author's main points?

4. Are the ideas arranged in a particular order?

5. Note the conclusion. How does it relate to the thesis?

   Does it adequately complete the essay? Explain.

6. List several words and phrases that describe the author's style.

7. What is your opinion of the essay?

Name ____________________ Date ____________

7-12. ON STAGE

An audience gets a vast amount of information about a play from the first glimpse of the stage as the curtain goes up. Choose a play from the era and set the stage for Act I. Below is the outline of the stage. Show the placement of furnishings, including doors and windows, and people. Place notes in the margins regarding lighting, sound effects, directions, or any other pertinent information for your particular play.

Title and author ____________________

AUDIENCE

Name ______________________________ Date ______________

7-13. NEW WORDS FOR NEW THINGS

Since World War II the changes occurring in American society have been breathtaking. Thousands of new words have been added to an already vibrant language to accommodate new products, discoveries, ideas, and methods of doing things.

DIRECTIONS: For each field, list four English words that did not exist, at least with their present meanings, before World War II. Put a check by those that were present in the literature of the era that you have read.

TRAVEL

1. ______________
2. ______________
3. ______________
4. ______________

BUSINESS

1. ______________
2. ______________
3. ______________
4. ______________

WAR/DEFENSE

1. ______________
2. ______________
3. ______________
4. ______________

SCIENCE/MEDICINE

1. ______________
2. ______________
3. ______________
4. ______________

NEW PRODUCTS

1. ______________
2. ______________
3. ______________
4. ______________

YOUR CHOICE

1. ______________
2. ______________
3. ______________
4. ______________

Name ______________________________ Date ______________

7-14. INTO THE FUTURE

Choose a favorite character from the literature of the era and project him or her twenty years into the future. First, describe briefly the society in which the character lives; in Part II describe his or her life, including such things as where he or she lives, friends, occupation, leisure activities. For Part III fill in information that fits the personality of the character, yet fits the time in which he or she lives, for example, beliefs, conflicts, emotions, and whatever else you feel would apply.

Character ______________________________ Date ______________

I. Society ______________________________

II. Outer life ______________________________

III. Inner life ______________________________

Name ______________________________ Date ________________

7-15. FISH OR FOWL

Literary works are classified according to types or categories, called *genres*. *Genre* is a French word meaning "kind" or "type." Biography, poetry, essay, short story, drama, and novel are some of the more general categories.

DIRECTIONS: Classify the selections in this section according to the genres listed.

NONFICTION

Biography/ Autobiography

1. ______________________
2. ______________________
3. ______________________

Poetry

1. ______________________
2. ______________________
3. ______________________
4. ______________________
5. ______________________
6. ______________________
7. ______________________

Essay or Speech

1. ______________________
2. ______________________
3. ______________________
4. ______________________

FICTION

Short Story

1. ______________________
2. ______________________
3. ______________________
4. ______________________
5. ______________________
6. ______________________

Drama

1. ______________________
2. ______________________
3. ______________________
4. ______________________

Novel

1. ______________________
2. ______________________
3. ______________________
4. ______________________

Name ______________________ Date ____________

7-16. REAL OR IMAGINED?

Science fiction is a form of fiction that has its basis in science, either factual or hypothetical. It is this basis that the author uses as a springboard to take us into the future or beyond scientific law or to another planet or dimension. Science fiction matured and attained respectability in the last part of the twentieth century; eminent authors and scientists work in the genre and use it not only to tell a good story, but to depict goals and values.

DIRECTIONS: Fill in the information asked for below for a science fiction novel or short story you have read.

Title and author ______________________

Characters—was there anything unusual about them? ______________________

____

____

Setting (time and place) ______________________

On the back of this page, summarize the plot in 150 to 175 words. Then, below, tell whether there were any unusual characteristics, for example, space travel, mental or physical phenomena, and so on. Was the plot sheer fantasy or a projection of the possible?

____

____

____

____

____

What social values does the author seem to admire? Explain your answer.

____

____

____

____

____

____

____

Name ______________________________ Date ______________

7-17. SEE AND TELL

Television is a major source of entertainment today. Programs, which originate as scripts, can be analyzed in much the same way as written literature. In fact, being an alert, critical observer can be rewarding.

DIRECTIONS: Choose a television program that tells a story, and answer the following questions. Use the back of this paper if you need more room for any of the answers.

Program title ______________________________

1. Plot pattern—tell what happens in the following parts

   a. Exposition ______________________________

   ____

   b. Narrative hook ______________________________

   c. Rising action (be brief) ______________________________

   ____

   ____

   d. Climax ______________________________

   e. Falling action ______________________________

   f. Resolution ______________________________

2. Setting a. Place ______________________________

   b. Time ______________________________

3. Characterization

   a. Main character(s) ______________________________

   b. Description ______________________________

   ____

   ____

4. Mood ______________________________

5. Theme ______________________________

Name ______________________________ Date ______________

7-18. IT ALL DEPENDS

As you know, the point of view from which an author chooses to tell a story determines the amount and type of information that is revealed. The point of view also helps determine the reader's attitude toward the characters.

DIRECTIONS: Copy the first five to ten lines of a short story or novel. Note the point of view. For Part II rewrite the sentences from a different point of view, then answer the two questions.

I. ORIGINAL VERSION

Title and Author ______________________________

Text ______________________________

____

____

____

____

Point of view ______________________________

II. New Version ______________________________

____

____

____

____

Point of view ______________________________

1. What do we *not* know in the first version that we know in the second?

2. What do we know in the first version that we do *not* know in the second?

Name ______________________________ Date ______________

7-19. THE PART IS THE WHOLE

Metonymy is a figure of speech that substitutes one thing for another to which it is closely related. For example, "the Crown" refers to a king or queen; "the White House" refers to the president of the United States. *Synecdoche* is a figure of speech that uses a part to represent the whole. For example, "a hired hand" means the whole hired person.

DIRECTIONS: From literature you have read, copy one example of metonymy and one example of synecdoche. Then write one more example of each. If you cannot remember a common example, make up an original one. Then explain what the figure of speech means.

METONYMY

1. a. Example from literature ______________________________

   ____

   b. Explanation ______________________________

   c. Source (title and author) ______________________________

2. a. Your example ______________________________

   b. Explanation ______________________________

SYNECDOCHE

1. a. Example from literature ______________________________

   ____

   b. Explanation ______________________________

   c. Source ______________________________

2. a. Your example ______________________________

   ____

   b. Explanation ______________________________

7-20. VOCABULARY LIST

1. abject
2. aboard
3. affinity
4. amble
5. annals
6. assiduous
7. banal
8. cacophony
9. capricious
10. clarity
11. concentric
12. confiscated
13. conglomeration
14. consort
15. continuity
16. continuum
17. couturier
18. cryptic
19. deride
20. elation
21. enmity
22. extol
23. fatuous
24. fiasco
25. gauche
26. genetic
27. glib
28. grotesque
29. haphazard
30. hobble
31. infuse
32. illusion
33. illusive
34. imminent
35. implacable
36. indolently
37. insidious
38. integrate
39. interpose
40. mastication
41. media
42. meditate
43. mesmerize
44. morose
45. mosaic
46. oblique
47. ominous
48. ostracize
49. paragon
50. parallels
51. pawns
52. pinnacle
53. pittance
54. placid
55. poignant
56. profusion
57. rapacity
58. repugnant
59. ribald
60. rue
61. scintilla
62. solstice
63. spectral
64. stoicism
65. superficial
66. symmetry
67. tenement
68. tenuous
69. transcendental
70. transubstantiation
71. tumult
72. ulterior
73. valid
74. verity
75. vestige

Name ________________________________ Date ________________

7-21. YOU DON'T SAY

This exercise will help you review the vocabulary words as well as some common compositional techniques.

DIRECTIONS: Write two sentences as examples of each of the following; use a vocabulary word in each.

1. A *statement of fact,* whether correct or incorrect, can be proven.

   a. ________________________________

   b. ________________________________

2. An *opinion* cannot be proven; you can only agree or disagree.

   a. ________________________________

   b. ________________________________

3. A *generalization* is a statement that is imprecise and vague.

   a. ________________________________

   b. ________________________________

4. A *cause-and-effect statement* states that one thing causes another.

   a. ________________________________

   b. ________________________________

5. An *either-or argument* says that there are only two possibilities.

   a. ________________________________

   b. ________________________________

6. *Parallelism* is the repetition of the same syntax within a sentence.

   a. ________________________________

   b. ________________________________

Name ______________________ Date ______________

7-22. THINK IT THROUGH

Analogies

1. Parallel : Intersecting ::
   A. Line : Oblique
   B. Field : Farm
   C. Fiasco : Success
   D. Placid : Calm
   E. Level : Even
2. Verity : Truthful ::
   A. Stoicism: Impassive
   B. Placid : Chaotic
   C. Field : Farm
   D. Pawns : Kings
   E. Blue : Green
3. Masticate : Food ::
   A. Solstice : Sun
   B. Clarity : Truth
   C. Valid : License
   D. Placid : Lake
   E. Hobble : Horse
4. Ominous : Storm cloud ::
   A. Pittance : Profusion
   B. Placid : Serene
   C. Tumult : Chaos
   D. Ulterior : Interior
   E. Cryptic : Message
5. Media : Newspaper ::
   A TV : Radio
   B. Mosaic : Tile
   C. Calm : Serene
   D. Crown : King
   E. Meditate : Zen
6. Banal : Ordinary ::
   A. Integrate : Separate
   B. Placid : Calm
   C. Farm : Field
   D. Sky : Earth
   E. Concentric : Square

Synonyms and Antonyms

You will find a synonym and an antonym answer for each word below. Mark the synonyms with an S and the antonyms with an A.

1. Oblique
   A. Indirect B. Straightforward C. Level D. Concentric E. Obligation
2. Deride
   A. Extol B. Transport C. Belittle D. Interpose E. Derail
3. Consort
   A. Scepter B. Husband C. Sister D. Stranger E. Kingdom
4. Ribald
   A. Hairless B. Puritanical C. Lewd D. Foreign E. Silly
5. Symmetry
   A. Measurement B. Balance C. Sympathy D. Illness E. Inharmony

Appendix

SUGGESTED AUTHORS

Section 1. The Colonial Era

William Bradford
Anne Bradstreet
William Byrd II
Christopher Columbus
Dekanawida
Jonathan Edwards
Sarah Kemble Knight
Robert de LaSalle
Cotton Mather
John Smith
Edward Taylor
Alvar Nunez Cabeza de Vaca

Section 2. The Revolution

Jean de Crèvecoeur
Benjamin Franklin
Philip Freneau
Patrick Henry
Thomas Jefferson
Thomas Paine
Phyllis Wheatley

Section 3. A New Literature

William Cullen Bryant
James Fenimore Cooper
Oliver Wendell Holmes
Washington Irving
Fanny Kemble
Henry Wadsworth Longfellow
James Russell Lowell
James Pennington
Edgar Allan Poe
John Greenleaf Whittier
Frances Wright

Section 4. Independence in Literature

Louisa May Alcott
Davy Crockett

Frederick Douglass
Ralph Waldo Emerson
Margaret Fuller
Nathaniel Hawthorne
Sidney Lanier
Robert E. Lee
Abraham Lincoln
Herman Melville
Harriet Robinson
Mollie Sanford
Chief Seattle
Elizabeth Cady Stanton
Harriet Beecher Stowe
Henry David Thoreau
Henry Timrod
Sojourner Truth

Section 5. Realism and Naturalism

Ambrose Bierce
Black Hawk
Kate Chopin
Stephen Crane
Emily Dickinson
W.E.B. Du Bois
Paul Laurence Dunbar
Mary W. Freeman
Hamlin Garland
Bret Harte
Helen Hunt Jackson
Henry James
Sarah Orne Jewett
Chief Joseph
Jack London
Edgar Lee Masters
M. N. Murfree
Edwin Arlington Robinson
Santanta
Mark Twain

Section 6. Social Change

Sherwood Anderson
W. H. Auden
Stephen Vincent Benet
Willa Cather
Countee Cullen
E. E. Cummings

John Dos Passos
T. S. Eliot
William Faulkner
F. Scott Fitzgerald
Robert Frost
Ernest Hemingway
Langston Hughes
Robinson Jeffers
Sinclair Lewis
Vachel Lindsay
Amy Lowell
Robert Lowell
Archibald MacLeish
Claude McKay
Edna St. Vincent Millay
Marianne Moore
Dorothy Parker
Katherine Anne Porter
Ezra Pound
John Crowe Ransom
Carl Sandburg
Upton Sinclair
Luther Standing Bear
John Steinbeck
Wallace Stevens
Jesse Stuart
Sara Teasdale
James Thurber
Jean Toomer
Margaret Walker
Eudora Welty
William Carlos Williams
Thomas Wolfe
Richard Wright

Section 7. Into the Future

Teresa Poloma Acosta
Alice Adams
Edward Albee
Maya Angelou
John Ashbury
Isaac Asimov
James Baldwin
Saul Bellow
Elizabeth Bishop

Ray Bradbury
Gwendolyn Brooks
Joseph Brodsky
Truman Capote
Rachel Carson
John Cheever
James Dickey
Joan Didion
Annie Dillard
E. L. Doctorow
Ralph Ellison
Gail Godwin
Rodolpho Gonzales
Lorraine Hansberry
Robert Hayden
Joseph Heller
Lillian Hellman
John Hersey
Garrison Keillor
Jack Kerouac
Maxine Kumin
Randall Jarrell
William Least Moon
Ursula LeGuin
Denise Levertov
Bernard Malamud
David Mamet
Carson McCullers
Larry McMurty
Jesus P. Melendez
Arthur Miller
James Masao Mitsui
N. Scott Momaday
Toni Morrison
Joyce Carol Oates
Flannery O'Connor
Eugene O'Neil
Simon Ortiz
Grace Paley
Sylvia Plath
Theodore Roethke
Philip Roth
Anne Sexton
Sam Shepard
Leslie Marmon Silko
Isaac Bashevis Singer

Gary Soto
Amy Tan
Anne Tyler
John Updike
Kurt Vonnegut, Jr.
Alice Walker
E. B. White
Richard Wilbur
Tennessee Williams
August Wilson

LITERARY TERMS INDEX